TO HELL
AND BEYOND

*The first enlisted man's version of what happened
as a Prisoner of War in Vietnam*

TO HELL AND BEYOND

*The first enlisted man's version of what happened
as a Prisoner of War in Vietnam*

The story of SSgt. Nathan B. Henry as told to

Beth W. Vinson

Mill City Press, Inc.
212 3rd Avenue North, Suite 570
Minneapolis, MN 55401
612.455.2294
www.millcitypublishing.com

ISBN - 1-934937-28-2
ISBN - 978-1-934937-28-0
LCCN - 2008939092

Cover Design by Jennifer Wheeler
Typeset by Peggy LeTrent

Printed in the United States of America

Table of Contents

Dedication

I would like to dedicate this book to my parents, Thurman and Arcilla Henry, because of the six years of worry they went through while I was a POW. The years that I was a captive was probably as bad or worse for them as it was for me because I knew I was alive but they didn't. My dad passed away on October 24, 1997, just as this book was being written. I would also like to dedicate this book to the families of the fifty-eight thousand men and women who gave the ultimate sacrifice and to the over 2,100 MIA's still unaccounted for.

SSgt. Nathan B. Henry
US Army–Retired

It has been an honor and a privilege to write this book and to get to know one of America's greatest silent heroes, Mr. Nat Henry. It is my hope that in writing his memoirs I was able to do justice to him and to the other POWs that served time in the hellholes of Vietnamese prisons. I would like to thank Mr. Henry for his patience in answering my endless questions and in spending his time to help me complete this book. I want to include a special dedication to my parents for their unending love and support over the years and to my "Sunshine," who has provided me with strength, courage, and a reason to go forward when no reason existed.

Lastly, to the courageous men and women of all military branches who fought in the Vietnam conflict. This book is dedicated to those who came home, to those who spent time as POWs, and, most importantly, to those who made the greatest sacrifice of all so we could remain free Americans. You have not been forgotten.

Beth W. Vinson
Author

Synopsis

In *To Hell and Beyond*, the hero didn't wear silver wings on his uniform, and no screaming-eagle made from steel propelled him into battle. He didn't belong to any Officer's Club, and only the basic ribbons of a foot soldier graced his broad chest. The one thing he *did* have, which continues still today, is a love for his country, his fellow Americans, and a will to live that goes beyond description. In his slow southern drawl, SSgt. Nathan Henry, US Army, (Ret.) related to me what it was like to spend 2,094 days struggling to stay alive while a POW in Vietnam. As far as we know, this is the first *enlisted* man's version of what happened during those gruesome years behind enemy lines.

I was raised in the same small country town as Nathan (Nat) Henry, and I know how deep his roots are planted in the ways of survival and country life that stems from living within the Blue Ridge Mountains of North Carolina. Time would reveal how the knowledge he gained while roaming these rugged hills digging ginseng and fishing for trout in the cold mountain creeks would help this young soldier endure the tortures and trials of being a Prisoner of War. It would be these same skills that would see him through a grueling forty-eight-day forced march on the Ho Chi Minh Trail, living in jungle cages for more than two years, and sustaining him long enough to eventually make it back to the southern home he so dearly loved.

To Hell and Beyond portrays the true story of torture, imprisonment, and the barbarous acts inflicted upon a man few people would ever

ix

know. He, and the other enlisted men who spent time as Prisoners of War, were not known to the general public simply because they weren't highly decorated pilots or thrust into the limelight during Operation Homecoming in 1973. This is the story of one man who defied all odds to survive and who, through recalling painful memories, will lead the reader step-by-step into the horrors and debilitation suffered by him and all our men while held as POWs during the Vietnam conflict. This manuscript, although based on one man, reveals the pride and determination of all POWs and their struggle to survive the tortures inflicted by the enemy in an effort to break their spirits and turn them against the country that had sent them to the Godforsaken jungles of Vietnam. This is the personal story of Nathan B. Henry and his journey *To Hell and Beyond*.

Introduction

"What are you gonna call it?" he asked, his hands fidgeting nervously, looking for something to do, searching his mind for the next thing to say. "To Hell and Beyond," I replied with a bit of cautious skepticism in my voice. Waiting with nervous anticipation, I wondered what thoughts were filling his mind during those few tense seconds that hung between us. Slowly his head turned in my direction. Those tired brown eyes staring deep into mine. No expression. No life. The lines of his weathered face were chiseled deep into the flesh, revealing a history that only he would ever really know. He had not only been to hell, but had lived it, breathed it, then finally escaped its clutches after almost six years. A POW in Vietnam, Staff Sergeant Nathan B. Henry, US Army (Ret.), had not only stared hell in the face; he had beaten it and lived to tell me his story twenty-four years later.

He stared at me for only a few brief seconds, then turned away as a slow grin spread across his face. A soft chuckle escaped his lips, then in a slow country drawl he said, "Yeah...I reckon that just about describes it." I was relieved, to say the least, and a bit more comfortable after winning his approval. The title would stay...I would listen and write...He would talk and remember. Eventually, we would both laugh, both shed tears, share the anxieties and pains of dredging up those memories once again. In the end, however, we both would gain knowledge...peace of mind...a sense of closure and a reason for being. Either way, a friendship and a bond would be established. A level of trust escalated for him, while an indescribable respect for the human spirit came from depths within me that I never knew existed. Together we relived the horrendous days and nights of a POW in Vietnam. This is a man who wanted only to serve his country then return home to the slow pace of his southern roots and live a quiet life nestled in the safety of these rugged mountains they call the Smokies. A man who suffered more from the torturous cavities recessed deep within our minds that we call a memory. A man who has been To Hell and Beyond.

Chapter One

Ground Pounders

Call them what you will: grunts, ground-pounders, foot soldiers. Some even prefer "rednecks," "uneducated," "common enlisted men." Whatever label you choose, there's one thing each of these men deserve, and that is the respect and undying gratitude of the American people for the sacrifices they made in Vietnam. These men didn't wear shiny bars and ribbons across their chests, nor did they have oak leaf clusters on their collars. They were not recognized as "those who gave their all" in the prison camps and came back as public heroes. What they *did* have, and still possess to this day, is an unbelievable depth of pride in their country, a love of their fellow Americans, and a spirit that could not be broken despite the horrendous and inhumane treatment forced upon them while Prisoners of War in Vietnam.

Enlisted men were considered uneducated and lacking in the ability to manipulate their captors as effectively as POW officers. On his own level, with or without extensive training, holding an eighth grade education or being an Ivy League scholar, a celebrated aviator or a private with a rifle, each man endured his own living hell at the hands of his captors. It matters not who was beaten more severely or deprived most often of nourishing food. It doesn't matter who was the SRO (Senior Ranking Officer) in camp, or whose cage in the jungle was smaller. Each man paid an extreme price for his service and loyalty to the United States of America, and each has his own set of deeply embedded scars that remain forever haunting from within. The memories alone have provided a hell on earth that most humans cannot begin to fathom or understand, let alone live and breathe each day as the gnawing ghosts claw at their remaining sanity.

We have all read the numerous accounts of hellish days in captivity for downed, high-ranking aviators, but seldom has the story been told of the common enlisted man and his fight for survival in the jungles of Vietnam. He didn't have a mind full of strategic plans of attack or maps that were memorized for pinpoint bombing raids. And maybe he didn't have the opportunity to attend POW survival training before being shipped to an unfamiliar and even more unfriendly country. His only equipment for survival was a fierce loyalty to America, a head that was filled with the ways of the military and what it expected of him, and a soul that would remain free despite the tortures inflicted by his enemy. The enlisted man was not highly decorated or known for giving speeches to great crowds, but he was far from common and needs to be remembered as such.

It seems the majority of military men I've met or read about were officers of some rank or other all with their own stories to tell. From Ensigns and Admirals, Lieutenants and Generals, even numerous Special Forces personnel, all have related to me their accounts of how they saw and experienced Vietnam from various levels of the fighting arena. I have the utmost respect and admiration for each and every man who pulled time in that ghastly jungle. But I, like so many people, tend to overlook the real backbone of any military operation--the enlisted man.

After the recent completion of my first book about a Navy SEAL, I had the great honor to be introduced to another man who was far removed from the glitz and glory of "Operation Homecoming" in February and March of 1973, staged by then President Nixon for the POWs held in Vietnam. In general, 591 captured Americans left Vietnam headed for their homes in the United States, of which 566 were military personnel. Of this entire group, only 59 were enlisted men, 11 were Marines, and 48 were Army personnel, respectively.

From a total of 26 Marines captured, 16 spent their time in jungle camps, while the total of 77 Army POWs were all kept in the jungles instead of the prison camps to the north in Hanoi, save a select few. Most of the jungle captives were eventually moved north after the death of Ho Chi Minh and for reasons of security when the U.S. began bombing in late 1969. Throughout captivity, though, the entire group of POWs was "top-heavy" with officers and aviators from the Navy and Air Force. Nevertheless, each man had his own story to tell or to keep to himself, as some have chosen. Yet, after having spent time with the man I will describe shortly, I found the days for an enlisted man were no better, and many times worse, than were those of the officers. Those stories will come a little later, though, because this man needs a proper and thorough introduction of his background and raising, as it contributes greatly to his overall story. I feel, too, that at least a little history of the system, in which he was forced to endure countless days at the hands of his captors, is necessary to understand his story.

From the text of the Nuremberg trials, military men were convicted for committing "war crimes" and "crimes against humanity." In 1949, North Vietnam had signed the Geneva Convention Relative to the Treatment of Prisoners of War. Along with three other countries, China, North Korea, and the Soviet Union, North Vietnam filed a reservation to Article 85. Their argument being that If a Nazi could not be protected by saying, "I was only following orders," then war criminals in the future could not hide behind the Geneva Convention, either. The Vietnamese viewed their American captives as criminals rather than Prisoners of War, so when a POW demanded his rights as stated in the Geneva Convention, he was met with a clear and concise statement of Articles 2 and 85. His captors did not recognize the Geneva agreements, therefore stating they were not bound by any law because the United States had invaded Vietnam in an undeclared aggression against their people and homeland. Acting under these interpretations, the Vietnamese considered their American captors as falling under the policy for criminals of war, not prisoners. Both Articles, along with the reservations filed by the Vietnamese, immediately cast all prisoners as criminals without protection under international law and brought guilty charges of high crimes against the Vietnamese people. As such, the prison camps became "political prisons," whereby its American hostages were used to alter their mindsets, or, for political purposes, as bargaining chips. After word reached the States that the Vietnamese were using our military men in its propaganda war, the United States government began an effort to convince the Vietnamese that following the provisions of the Geneva Convention would be in their best interest. While these efforts were valiant, they were lacking in effort and very slow to take effect. In the meantime, our men were learning the painful truth about reality within their own confines.

The goal of the North Vietnamese captors was to force the Americans to abandon their former allegiances and obey the oppressive administrative authority. Rules were developed for these political prisons and given to the American captives. Following the same rules developed by the Chinese during the Korean War, the North Vietnamese determined that punishment would come first, with the proposed violation to be defined later. Two types of violations occurred within the camps: "discipline" and "system." "Discipline" violations encompassed such charges as organizing escapes, spreading rumors, remaining imperialistic, or defecating in their pants as a result of dysentery. This particular act was seen by the camp authorities as an attempt by the Americans to destroy their clothing, and, therefore, was a punishable act. "System" violations were described as the use of books or magazines as toilet paper or wraps for cigarettes, holding unauthorized discussion sessions, communications between cells, or any activity that altered the acceptable "daily life" schedule. However, if anything other than what the camp authority wanted ensued, then it became a violation with the guarantee of punishment soon to follow.

The Code of Conduct. A military man's creed. Name, rank, serial number, and date of birth, became known as the "Big Four." Words a man could live by, and as the war in Vietnam proved no different from others, words to die by. Although the Vietnamese followed the examples of the Chinese on how to run a political prison, they took the examples one step farther by carefully studying the Code of Conduct established by the American military. As early as 1963, the Vietnamese were able to understand and recite back to their POWs the exact content and honorable intentions of the "Code." In later years, however, prisoners began hearing the rumor that the Code was useless, opposed by the American people, and would be changed by a new government as directed by the people when Nixon took office in November of 1968. An excellent strategy of the camp authorities was to give American POWs their own hard-line interpretation of the Code. They told the prisoners that if they gave a single piece of information other than the Big Four, then the Code had already been violated and further cooperation with camp authorities would be in the prisoners' best interests. Stating this interpretation, coupled with endless torture and abuse, obtained the information the Vietnamese wanted in many situations. Personal histories, oral or written confessions, whether true or false, appeals to other prisoners, propaganda broadcasts or recordings, or any other communications on behalf of the enemy or critical or harmful to the United States and/or persons affiliated with the same was considered a violation of the Code and a victory for the camp authority.

Despite threats and tortures, the American captives relished their own small victory against their captors by clinging to the established Code in several ways. Many prisoners battled the camp authority by writing or broadcasting statements that were so false and erroneous that interpretation of same often brought a moment of humor to fellow inmates. Minor "victories" such as these increased morale among the Americans and kept their spirits strong. These stories and writings, though totally fictitious, were believable by the North Vietnamese and therefore, more frequently than not, satisfied their demands. What frustrated the Vietnamese was their own inability to coerce information they felt critical to their own war efforts. As many former POWs have cited in their memoirs, the enemy had numerous methods for extracting any military secret they desired. The only drawback, fortunately for our men, was that the camp authorities didn't know the right questions to ask.

The main thrust for most American prisoners for holding out information was their loyalty to each other. Faith in God and the Code was essential and an endless supply of strength from which to draw during horrendous torture sessions. But above all was the need to return from interrogation and be able to look a fellow prisoner in the eye with both men knowing the limits had been met with utmost resistance. The first time each man was "broken"

7

by his captors, the majority reported an overwhelming guilt that swept over their agonized bodies in a pain more excruciating than the physical beatings they had just endured. A feeling of betrayal to their country, to their military honor, and to their own self-respect, let alone the feeling of betrayal of their fellow prisoners, was gut-wrenching and mentally devastating. The men felt no punishment could be more harsh than losing the respect of his peers and giving more information than the Big Four allowed. The obligation to withhold additional information kept most American prisoners hanging on through some of the worst torture sessions until they reached the point of collapsing. Once the communication process started, however, the newly captured prisoners learned that everyone before them had been broken, and each subsequent captive would eventually break under the severe extraction methods. This information from previous captors erased the self-inflicted pain to some extent, while time and learning the ways of a Prisoner of War would eventually heal the rest. The men had all done their best to withhold information, and that was all anyone could expect.

The "Hanoi Hilton," as the main camp in North Vietnam was called, provided unbelievable living conditions. Placement within its walls became more of a test for survival than a prison, and numerous Americans never escaped the block walls and stench of the "Hilton." The dark, dank cells that contained our men were barely large enough for one man, yet often times as many as four prisoners were forced into a cell approximately five feet by eight feet with one "personal bucket" to be shared by all. Each man was given a woven reed mat upon which to lie, and if he was lucky and complied with requests from the authorities, he received a single sackcloth blanket to wrap in against the bone-chilling winds of winter. More often than not, the cells were infested with rats and other crawling creatures and had no windows or light to dispel the bleak loneliness within. The doors were usually heavy wooden structures with a metal peephole, which remained shut unless a guard opened it for viewing the prisoners or delivering food. The prisoners were allowed to leave the room, if compliance was satisfactory, once a day to bathe in cold water and clean their personal buckets or wash their clothes. Many times, however, the men would remain in their cells for days on end without light, fresh water, baths, or fresh air to cleanse their lungs and lighten their spirits. Some cells had a single light bulb that hung suspended from the rafters above, but was only allowed to be turned on during certain times of the day, while in others the light emitted a dim glow twenty-four hours a day.

Food containers consisted of a water jug for each man, a tin or wooden bowl for the little food they received, and sometimes a tin cup for drinking. Their daily meals consisted mainly of a watery green soup with little or no measurable contents. Called "sewer greens," this green, leafy weed, similar to water lilies, was a wild plant that flourished among the slime and algae in the waste ponds surrounding the camps and was used to make the soup. The greens were foul tasting and tough, but became somewhat of a treat when small pieces were found floating in the broth. On occasion, a rare delicacy was discovered in the soup, which might consist of a piece of fat meat, a drowned roach or bug of some kind, or a small piece of vegetable. The soup would be accompanied by a little chunk of bread or a very small portion of rice and served only twice a day around noon and early evening. No other nourishment was available throughout their endless days of captivity. For the lucky prisoners, an American holiday would bring a feast to their starving bodies. The camp authorities would have some type of meat, usually wild turkey, canned pork, or gibbon (monkey) prepared for their meals. In addition to the meat, the prisoners were provided with a piece of vegetable, extra bread or rice, and, on occasion, a piece of fruit or a morsel of hard candy or chocolate. To their starving tongues, these meals were fit for a king, and they ate ravenously, but the end result almost always invoked a severe case of dysentery or diarrhea. Within a day or two after these meals, the personal buckets of each cell would be overflowing and crawling with maggots or tapeworms passed by the men. Regardless of their efforts, the American prisoners suffered continuously with internal worms, infections, and bodily functions that shut down from lack of proper nourishment. After a short period of time in captivity, it became an effort in survival just to retain any positive effects from the meals they received.

Living conditions for those POWs kept in the jungle camps were even worse. An assortment of "cells" existed depending upon the location of the camp and the severity of punishment rendered, or was simply determined by the desires of the camp commander. The typical jungle hut was a bamboo structure, usually built low to the ground in the shape of a lean-to, where the poles were tied together with hemp vines or thin strips of bamboo. When the sun dried out the strips, camp guards would pour water on the bindings to make them swell and prevent the poles from becoming loose. The roof was most often covered with palm fronds or was a thatch-roofed from elephant grass. There was also a "gate" of sorts affixed to the front of the structure and was locked and/or interlaced with barbwire to prevent escape. In these particular structures, the bare ground was the flooring. In certain instances, the prisoners were given a woven mat to lay on the ground and usually a mosquito net to hang over them at night, but these were pure luxury items to many. The average dimensions of this particular unit were approximately four to five feet wide and about three feet tall on the high end, while running to the ground on the other.

One of the greatest hazards for the captives was the animals that had easy access to the lean-tos. Snakes were plentiful in the jungles, especially two deadly varieties of the cobra family. The Vietnamese considered snake meat a delicacy and had great pleasure when the slimy creatures would find the warm bodies of our men and crawl into their huts. If one of the prisoners would start screaming about a snake, many times the guards would start running, then just stand and laugh at the terror of the man who was trapped. Eventually, when the snake left the hut, the Vietnamese would kill it and share in a feast for dinner. In addition to the snakes, poisonous spiders and lizards, biting ants, the endless supply of mosquitoes, rats, and, of course, leeches, plagued the men on a daily basis.

A second type of structure used in the jungles was a bamboo cage supported on stilts. This particular cell was made completely of bamboo poles and was rectangular in shape. The dimensions were approximately three by four by eight feet, yet designed where the occupant could sit up but not stand. The men in these structures seldom had the protection of a mosquito net and rarely even had a mat to lie upon. These "boxes" were normally used during times of harsh punishment. Although not always the case, in most circumstances, the men were not allowed out of these cages for anything. They defecated through the slats of bamboo, were not allowed to bathe for months on end, and were only allowed out to clean the urine from beneath the box. This was a practice that didn't happen very often, either, so the men would sit above their own waste for weeks on end.

Probably the most cruel and inhumane device used to house prisoners was "the cage." This particular unit was also made entirely of bamboo and then suspended from tree limbs so it hung about three feet above the ground. Smaller than the other units, the cage was normally three by three by four feet. Within these confines, many of the Americans, being large in size compared to the Vietnamese, didn't have enough room to sit down completely, nor could they stand upright. After months of this cramped confinement, the prisoners frequently lost the use of their legs due to a lack of proper circulation. Those men unfortunate enough to be held captive in this manner many times sustained permanent damage to their limbs. No mosquito nets were given, and certainly no other "luxuries" were available to these prisoners. Despite the severity of the cage itself, a favorite pastime for the guards was to twist and swing the cage endlessly as a form of torture. Another favorite was to jab the trapped men inside with sharpened sticks or rap on the bamboo back and forth with a stick or baton each time they passed. When the camp decided to move to another location, the men in the cages were forced to carry or drag their "houses" through the jungle, despite their deteriorated physical conditions. The only exception to this would come if a prisoner was so near death that he, too, had to be carried.

"Charlie" was very effective in his methods of torture. Many times when a man refused to reveal the desired information to the Viet Cong (VC), he would be tortured in front of the others in the hopes that seeing the cruel punishment to a fellow American would force someone else to talk. The prisoners were beaten severely with bamboo sticks, rifle butts, and tree limbs. They would be burned by hot coals from a smoldering fire, have their fingernails pulled out, or, if they were caught trying to pass information, their hands would be stomped severely by Charlie's feet until they were crushed and rendered useless. With the feet of prisoners locked securely in stocks, the VC would beat them constantly for sheer pleasure, usually breaking the bones and crippling the prisoners for months and even years. Other forms of torture included having the men tied in ropes that wrapped around their ankles, looped over their necks, then tied to their wrists while their arms were behind their backs. After being securely tied, the men were often times suspended from a hook or other device and hung upside down, which placed their bodies in excruciating pain for hours on end. Also while being held in the "ropes," the Vietnamese guards would frequently twist the men's arms or press them further past their heads to inflict even more pain. After prolonged exposure to the ropes, the arms and hands of the prisoners would lose all circulation, and their limbs would turn black and become numb. Although the numbness was a relief at times, the POW then dreaded having the ropes removed, as feeling would return to their limbs, and the excruciating pain would begin again. Many prisoners still retain the scars of the cutting ropes and have limited use or nerve damage even today.

Some captives even reported being buried alive, exposing only their neck and head to the multitudes of mosquitoes and biting ants that covered their raw flesh, and left in this condition for days on end. Other men were locked in solitary confinement for months, even years, without any word from another fellow prisoner. Solitary usually meant no light at all, no baths, very little food, and certainly no exercise from the tiny black cells in which they were kept. The varieties of tortures were unlimited, and in most situations, even beyond belief.

I've come to realize from conversations with others concerning the conditions of imprisonment of our military personnel in Vietnam that the general public seriously has no clue as to the severity of treatment those men received. They wrinkle their noses and listen with bated fascination to the grim details. Statements follow the quick history lesson such as "Oh, how awful," and "I can't imagine living like that." Concern is shown for these ex-POWs, hearts go out to them for the pain and suffering they endured, but, in the end, does it really matter? You're damned right it does!

The supreme sacrifice an individual can bestow upon his country and its inhabitants is his life. More than fifty-eight thousand men gave their lives during the Vietnam conflict, and even one life, in this writer's opinion, was too much. We can add, however, another 566 names to this list. These are names of all military POWs who served time in prison camps and were later released, because they, too, gave their lives to this country and the American people. Yes, they're alive and living throughout the four corners of this nation, but what kind of life has it been? Every single day since their release, these men have endured the nightmares and painful memories that have plagued their every waking moment. They bravely wear smiles upon their faces, laugh with their families and friends, and overall have led a pretty normal life... at least to the peering eyes of others. But what we, the masses, as free people within the United States, do not understand is that beyond the smiles and laughs of these gallant men lies the smoldering remains of ghosts too real to comprehend. While the rest of us take for granted the simple pleasures of freedom afforded to us by this great nation, we simply *must* remember our POWs and Veterans from *all* wars and the sacrifice of their own lives for our freedom. Not a single man who saw and confronted the enemy on a battlefield and returned in the end has remained untouched by his experiences. The cost, be it great or small, left its mark on these men, and there it will forever remain until their last breath is drawn. Inasmuch, we, the American people, until *our* last breath is drawn, should try to understand these sacrifices and thank God that when the Call to Arms is heralded, the best men in the world answer the call.

Chapter 2

Home Boys

As you enter the quiet still of the Burningtown Community and see the rugged mountains that loom all around, you can't help but feel safe as their forested arms reach out and gather you within their protecting slopes. Many years ago, I had the good fortune to work with Mrs. Arcilla Henry, who introduced me to this community on our many home visits, during which she related a good deal of the area's history. It seemed ironic to me that many years later I would be talking with her again, but this time it would be about her POW son, a subject clearly painful and troublesome to this day.

Burningtown, as Mrs. Henry explained to me years ago, received its name when the white soldiers invaded this secluded valley in 1838, under the direction of President Andrew Jackson, and proceeded to drive out the Native Americans who inhabited the surrounding area. The villages were pillaged and plundered by the invaders, while the people were gathered together to be moved west to Oklahoma. As the chief of the village looked for the last time upon his beloved homeland, great fires leapt from the ground consuming his home. With a single tear escaping down his weathered face, he uttered the words, "They're burning the town." The old chief then turned and was marched with the rest of his people for many days away from his home, his life, and the land, which had been so plentiful and gracious. The name "Burningtown" stuck, and has forever since been used to identify this small piece of paradise located deep within the heart of the Great Smoky Mountains. This quiet community is one of the few places left where native trout still swim lazily in the bubbling creeks, and where a drink from the mountain springs that abound can refresh a body's soul with one swallow.

On this clear summer day, a light breeze gently ruffles the leaves on the branches of trees that line both sides of this narrow country road I travel. Flickers of bright sunlight stream through the limbs and dance across my face, forcing a smile despite the slightly nervous feeling in my stomach. As I reach my destination, a sprawling, grey country house is nestled within beds of brightly colored flowers and a well-manicured lawn. I had met Nat once before and had established a great respect for him in the short amount of time we had spent together. Today, however, I would come to know more about the man who served almost six years within the torturous hands of the North Vietnamese, and then try to put his experiences into words.

Nathan Barney Henry was born on May 13, 1947, the youngest of three children belonging to Thurman and Arcilla Henry. The home where Nat spent his childhood days is still standing across the road from where he lives now and is the roof under which his now widowed mother still resides. Nat, as he is known by his friends, along with his brothers Pratt, the oldest, and Harry, the middle son, spent countless days in their youth roaming the mountainsides and fording the numerous streams around their homeland. Like other kids growing up, the Henry boys played 'Cowboys and Indians,' went camping, and, for the most part, learned the ways of survival for a quiet life in the country. Nat loved to fish more than anything, and when chores were done, he would grab his pole, dig a few worms, and head off to one of the nearby creeks. For years Nat and his brothers romped through the thick rhododendron, climbed the steep faces of the surrounding mountains, and learned the ways of the land. Ironically, the basic skills of survival he learned as a boy would later contribute to Nat's survival in the jungles of Vietnam.

There is no power on earth greater than a mother's love, and no force known to man that can break the bond between a mother and her child. A mother bears an incredible load where many fear to tread, yet the gentle embrace of her arms can calm and bring peace to the most frightened of hearts. She is the rock and strength of her family, sheds tears where no one else can see, and welcomes home even the most wayward child with an incredible depth of love and compassion. Men go off to war fighting to protect their country, while women stay behind praying for the protection of their men. It's never easy to watch a loved one leave home to fight in some godforsaken land, but when a mother sends her son, a piece of her goes with him, leaving a hollow ache that is indescribable.

After talking with Mrs. Henry, I now have a better understanding of what Nat's family endured during the years he was a Prisoner of War in Vietnam. Sergeant Henry was not the only one who suffered extreme torture at the hands of the enemy; Mrs. Henry was surviving her own living hell at home. Through a strong belief in God, support from other POW families, and by depending on sheer determination and will, Mrs. Henry never gave up hope that her son was still alive. A mother's instinct reassured her beliefs that one day he would be delivered once again to her waiting arms on free, American soil.

When asked what Nat enjoyed doing as a little boy, Mrs. Henry replied, "Well, they played all the time, but I would never let them play war games. I thought about that so much. Then all three of them was in service. I couldn't stand it," she continued. "Just all that old running and hollerin.' and Nick Rowland was the worst, and I'd ask him to be quiet. I didn't like all that noise and killin'. I let 'em play anything else though. I let 'em play Indians. They played that a lot, but I didn't want them to play war games!"

"They liked to go camping," Mrs. Henry recalled. "There was an old house over on the head of Rhinehart, and they would take loads of stuff to eat. They borrowed their sleeping bags from the Ag [agriculture] boys and they'd build a big, roaring fire in the fireplace and sit and tell tall tales. They started this camping about the time Nat went into high school. A lot of times I would take him and one [other] boy over there and leave them, and then go back after them the next day or the next afternoon." After a short pause Mrs. Henry continued recalling some of the camping trips. "I usually cooked everything for them to take. I kept thinking they was taking more than they could eat, but I'd bake a big cake of cornbread, and they would take maybe homemade soups. They could cook on the fireplace a little, but that's kind of hard."

"One time it was turning real cold and we was a-packing their stuff in a pickup truck. I think Chester Sorrells was with them, and he had the truck. I put them in a bunch of kindlin', and then I just went back to the woodshed and got a handful of pine knots, you know, and stuck them in there, too. When the boys came back, Nat said, 'Well, Mother, we would never have made it if it hadn't been for them pine knots!' Pine knots burn quick, you know." We both laughed heartily at the retelling of the story.

In early 1966, Pratt Henry, Nat's oldest brother, joined the National Guard. On June 13, 1966, the second oldest son, Harry, was sent to Fort Benning, Georgia, for Army basic training, then was transferred to Fort Stuart, Georgia. Nat, the youngest, soon followed with his enlistment in the Army in September of the same year. How difficult it must have been for Mr. and Mrs. Henry to see all three of their children in the service while the fighting in Vietnam escalated. How great a price must one family pay in service to their country and fellow Americans? The Henry family, in the end, paid an exorbitant amount.

"Pratt went in first," Mrs. Henry explained. "He was the oldest. Then Harry. But, you see, if Harry hadn't been in a car accident at Fort Stuart, Georgia, Nat wouldn't of had to gone. Harry was going to get plane reservations or going to see about something, I don't remember now, but they was in a convertible. They was three of them, and they come around a curve and hit a house. One boy hit the top of the house, and Harry was thrown over the house and into a swamp. The one that was driving was killed instantly. Harry said when he come to that he could see lights everywhere, and he was trying to get to the light. When he came out of the swamp, his clothes was tore off of him, and he was just bleeding something awful! Then someone said, 'Here's the ambulance, we're gonna put you in it.' Then (Harry) said, 'No, I'll just ride up front.' But when he reached for the door he didn't make it 'cause he passed out." Mrs. Henry laughed at her son's stubbornness then continued on. "He was in the hospital for I don't know *how* long, so he didn't get to go to Vietnam then, but he went when he heard Nat was missing. I was proud they was able to go, but I didn't want 'em all to have to go."

In May of 1966, Nathan Henry turned nineteen years old. By

17

September of the same year, he was drafted into the United States Army with a draft number of "2." Within days, Nat boarded a bus in the nearby town of Franklin headed for Knoxville, Tennessee, to be sworn into the military. Nat and the other new recruits were placed in the local YMCA for their first night away from home and were given their entrance exams and physicals. Around 4:00 p.m., on September 8, 1966, he took his oath, then was placed back on the bus headed for Fort Campbell, Kentucky. Off-loading from the bus, many of the green recruits immediately lit a cigarette and were just as quickly instructed to extinguish their smokes. "I got off the bus, lit a cigarette, then threw it on the ground," Nat stated through his laughter. "And, hell, I was doing pushups and hadn't been there ten minutes!"

After a week of orientation, the new recruits were assigned to their company posts and basic training began. Nat met Paul Davis, who had lived just outside Knoxville, Tennessee, and had been inducted the same day. They ended up in the same barracks during boot camp, where they soon became close friends. It was now November 1, 1966, and after six weeks of basic training, Nat was sent straight to Fort Polk, Louisiana, for AIT (Advanced Infantry Training). Because of the heavy fighting in Vietnam and the urgent need for fresh troops, no leave was given to the men after basic, as was customary. Paul and Nat rode the bus together, and, as they entered the gates to Fort Polk, a small sign posted on the entrance read: "Little Vietnam." They knew instantly what their future held.

After spending about seven weeks at Fort Polk in intensive training for jungle conditions, the two men were given fifteen days leave at Christmas. Another five weeks would finish out their training at Polk, and then it would be a flight to Oakland in California to await shipment to Vietnam. Nat and Paul decided to rent a hotel room on their first night in Oakland and enjoy some of the local establishments. Nat was still under the legal age limit, but they wanted to down a few beers on one of their last nights in the States. After asking Nat how hungover he was the next morning, his only reply was a soft laugh and these words: "Hell, I got kicked out before I got through the door!" So much for a planned evening on the town.

Two days later, the new recruits left Oakland for the short trip to

Travis Air Force Base, where they boarded a C-141 headed for Saigon, which had stops in Hawaii and Wake Island, then eighteen hours later arrived at Ben Wa. I asked Nat what his first thoughts were of Vietnam, and he replied, "I thought, 'Damn, what a country!'" It was now February 18, 1967. The men were placed in a holding camp at Ben Wa as the Replacement Company for the 191st. They stayed at this location for about a week before being sent to the 4th Infantry base camp at Pleiku. During the first few days there, the troops received in-country orientation, practiced search and destroy missions, and general familiarization with the country and enemy movements. "Pretty soon they put us on a chopper and sent us off to our Companies," Nat reflected. "Well, hell, we never been on a chopper, you know, and they pick up and start to turn sideways... You can't fall out, but everybody was holding on for dear life! Course I was put on the outer edge on one side, and it didn't have no doors, and when he lifted up....and they...hell!"

After spending a week at Ben Wa, the new recruits were sent to their firebases, where they were assigned to specific platoon and squad units. Nat and his friend Paul were separated at this point, with Nat assigned to the 4th Infantry Division while Paul was sent to the 1st Cavalry. One morning everyone was moved, being told they were now in Combat Assault, where they were loaded on Chinooks and placed in different firebases close to the 4th Infantry base camp. The first firebase, Lay LZ, in which Nat landed, was "hot." This was the second day in the field, and already they were in the thick of fighting the North Vietnamese. "You had to be in-country for thirty days and/or see action the first time out to get the CIB (Combat Infantry Badge), so, hell, I got mine in the first two days," Nat grinned as he spoke and shook his head in disbelief.

In his own words, Nat recalled his first impression of his field assignment. "The firebase, itself, was an old firebase and had already been cleared. They had used napalm and everything else on it, and [it] was just out in the middle of nowhere. The vegetation was all dead, but the perimeter way out around it was still green. The camp consisted of nothing but foxholes. We built bunkers, and that was it. We stayed a week in the firebase, and there was three companies of us. B Company would stay in the firebase for a week, then A Company would come in, and we'd go back out in the field with

19

C Company. There was always one company at the firebase, with the other two on search and destroy missions. I remember my first CO in the field was Captain Sherrill, and my platoon leader was Lieutenant Hasket."

Back at home, Mr. and Mrs. Henry kept in touch with their son as best as they could. "He wrote home every week, I guess," Mrs. Henry recalled, "Course I wrote him every other day and sent box after box of stuff to him. I would put candies and raisins and stuff that you knew would keep over there....and cigarettes," she laughed. "He would say, 'Well, I can get cigarettes over here, Mother,' but I would put 'em in anyway. Then when I knew he was in combat, we would send Kool-Aid and stuff like that so he could carry that with him. I got lots of letters from him before he got captured, and then after he was captured, we sent him stuff, too. The Army Department in Washington sent us a list, and we could send just so much stuff and so many pounds. Every three months I think it was."

Going from the lush, green mountains of Western North Carolina to the triple canopy jungles of Vietnam was a drastic change for Nat Henry. A world of strange sights, unusual smells, and frightening sounds lay in waiting, as would a monster with jaws opened wide that is luring its unsuspecting prey closer to death. A world where the morning mist quietly inhabited a serene landscape would later be lifted, only to reveal and invoke fear and terror into the hearts of men in combat. A world away from the quiet charm of his country home, the jungles and rice paddies of Vietnam were about to claim the innocent life of yet another victim and forever change the path of his destiny.

Chapter 3

Pleiku

Pleiku is located near the Ia Drang Valley. On November 15, 1965, the 1st Cavalry Division began to endure what became an agonizing thirty-four-day campaign in this valley, located in the Central Highlands of South Vietnam. It was a costly battle that took the lives of 234 young Americans, who fought and died together defending Landing Zones X-Ray and Albany. Altogether in following skirmishes, 305 gallant men lost their lives in that valley of death and forever changed the paths of history in Vietnam. This particular battle brought two armies together, where the leaders of the United States military would soon realize just how opposing the NVA were against our own forces.

The Ia (River) Drang Valley, nicknamed "The Iron Triangle," was remote and inaccessible by road and had long been a Communist sanctuary and infiltration route into the Central Highlands. A simple patrol became an all day struggle for the men who had to use machetes to hack their way through the tangled mass of vines and undergrowth that made every step arduous and painful. The area was filled with huge, sun-baked ant hills, steep ravines, nipa palms and elephant grass, and scrub brush that clawed at the troops as they tried to progress forward on their missions. "It was a lot like the mountains around here," Nat said. "You could get up on top of a ridge and maybe walk a little ways, and then you was right back into climbing up again. If you did get off into a little cove or something, you just had to chop your way through."

"In the six months in Vietnam, I had made around twenty combat assaults." Nat stated. "One platoon always went in first. I will never forget the first assault I made. It was my second day in the field. My platoon was the first to go in and it was 'hot,' which meant we had enemy contact. I can't remember his name, but my squad leader was killed after we had secured the area. We would set up our perimeter and build our bunkers. We had made the assault early that morning and had most of our bunkers done by late that afternoon, when we came under a mortar attack. We had a few men hit by shrapnel, and that evening I was hit in the head with a small piece, but didn't have to go in. When we would make an assault, we would set up a firebase, then the company that made it would stay a week. Then one of the other companies would come relieve us, and then they would stay a week. There were times when it would be ten to fifteen days, but it was always rotated between three companies."

The main threat to Pleiku province was in the western region close to the Cambodian border. While activity by the 1st North Vietnamese Division along the border had dropped sharply, intelligence sources detected a marked increase in enemy activity, particularly between Duc Co and the Ia Drang Valley. This particular sector was under the charge of the 4th Division's 2nd Brigade, who arranged for two B-51 strikes in the area on July 10th. Lt. Col. Corley J. Wright, commander of the 1st Battalion, 12th Infantry, had drawn the assignment of determining the results of these two strikes. A favorite tactic of the enemy after these bombing strikes was to send forces to the vicinity to ambush American units, who were out to assess the damage from the bombing runs, and Lt. Col. Wright was cautious with his approach to the task before him.

July 11, 1967, the day after the B-52 bombing strikes, had brought a lot of activity. Both B and C Companies had walked artillery on all four sides of their units that day as they conducted their search and destroy patrols. While one company took up a position on the fringe of the B-52 strikes, another entered the target area, but found little more than bomb craters. Both companies then moved east to establish separate perimeters a mile apart, amid the wooded, rocky hills just five miles from the Cambodian border. "My God," Nat said, "they was trails everywhere. I mean you could 'bout smell 'em, and when we set up that night, we just set up a perimeter. We were under-strength because all the old guys had rotated back to the States, and we were walking right through where the 1st Cavalry had been in a major fight back in '65." Additional caution by Lt. Col. Wright was fueled by the fact that the field strength of his companies had shrunk well below a hundred men each. After many of his troops had rotated back to the United States, completing their one-year tours, the rotation policy had brought in a large number of non-commissioned and company-grade officers inexperienced in combat.

"About three weeks before we were captured, we set up a perimeter that night, and one of the perimeter guards heard some noise in the bush. They ended up capturing three dinks, and when they wouldn't talk during interrogation, some of the guys took them up in a chopper and figured they would get them to talk one way or the other. They pushed two of 'em out, and then the third one started talking. I wasn't in the chopper that done that, but it was still our unit. He [the VC captive] said they knew where we was, and they also knew the old guys were rotating out and that we were under strength. He said, 'We're gonna wax you as quick as they get rotated.' They were right... I sent the last guy in [on rotation] the night before we got captured."

The morning of July 12, 1967, was like any other. Hot and humid, with a dense fog that engulfed the company perimeters; the air filled with annoying mosquitoes; cold C-rations again for breakfast and a long day ahead of patrolling through enemy territory. The mood was rather light, though, as the next day Company B would be returning to the firebase and would have a week to rest and catch up on much needed sleep. Due to the heavy blanket of fog, Lt. Col. Wright ordered a delay of the planned patrol and instead ordered both companies to conduct close-in patrols of the area.

"We got what they called fours and fives ever so often in the field, which was beer and Cokes," Nat said. "I think at headquarters you paid $10 a month, and you got two beers and two Cokes.... You didn't get them every day, though. You just got 'em whenever a chopper could bring 'em in. I was the only one that drank beer, so I'd swap my Cokes for all their beer. It was that old Korean beer, anyway, and it [was] hot, but.... I'll never forget, though, I drank one of them right before we left. I had two left in my pack, and I said to myself, 'Hell, I'm gonna drink a beer before I go out.' So that's what I did, and that was breakfast for me. Course, with all of it, you couldn't get drunk off of it... I think it was like 3.2 and wasn't much of a beer. It would quench a thirst anyhow."

A patrol consisting of a platoon from Company C became disoriented in the fog that morning and strayed about seven hundred meters from the perimeter. They encountered a squad of North Vietnamese troops, opened fire, and killed three, while the rest fled south in the direction of Company B's position. "That next morning they sent out, I think it was the 3^d platoon they sent out, and my God, they hadn't been gone ten minutes when they called back and said they was being overrun. The rest of the company then moved out to try and go get our platoon, but then we got hit before we got to 'em in an L-shaped ambush.... So they got us, too." The initial platoon consisted of eighteen to twenty men, leaving the company with about sixty-five men for support— a figure far short of the 240 plus men that comprise a regular company. "I was the RTO (Radio-Telephone Operator) for the 'Old Man,' or Company Commander, back in Headquarters." The CO (Commanding Officer) was new and had only been with B Company two or three weeks. He had been in Saigon, but wanted to get his CIB and had asked to be transferred to field operations.

By mid-morning, Company B had tried to establish radio contact with the lost platoon and direct them back to where Company B was waiting. Company C had spotted thirty soldiers of the 22nd North Vietnamese Army northeast of their perimeter and braced for an attack. When the attack failed to materialize, B's Company Commander ordered one of the platoons from his company to find the lost platoon from that morning and bring them back. Before the link-up could take place between the two platoons, an enemy force took Company C's platoon under fire, and by mid-morning, the platoon was virtually surrounded. This maneuver then left both companies with an unknown force of enemy soldiers caught between them.

Not knowing their exact locations, Lt. Col. Wright then requested artillery and mortar fire to be placed around Company C's platoon, then used helicopters to lift Company A from the firebase and placed them into the battle area. Wright then got a helicopter for himself shortly before 11:00 a.m. and began to direct the action from the air.

Once the enemy discovered that the platoon of Company B was also alone, they attacked them immediately. Under heavy enemy small arms and mortar fire, Company C was trying desperately to hold their position, but by now they had been completely surrounded by the 66th North Vietnamese Army. Lt. Col. Wright gave the orders for the remaining members of both companies to move to the support of their isolated platoons, while he would try to direct their movements from helicopter, by means of smoke grenades set off by the companies as they progressed. Company B had hardly set out when enemy mortar fire struck the command group, killing the company commander.

"When we moved out, I was trying to call the lead platoon, and the last words we got was 'We're overrun.' And that was the last communications I had. But then about that time they [the NVA] shot the receiver out of my hand, anyway. That's how lucky I was. I was on the radio, and they shot it out and shot the radio off my back. I was lucky 'cause they was coming this way and hitting the sides of it.... 'Cause I know damn well an AK-47 round would of gone straight through it." Nat paused for a long time and I sat quietly observing his expressions as he reflected on that morning, then he continued. "But we was caught in what they called the 'L-shaped' ambush. They had already set it up, plus was a-coming, and had even tied themselves up in trees. I shot two or three as they was tied up there with that old hemp vine."

As the battle progressed, men everywhere were screaming and dropping like dead flies. Total chaos, seemingly hours long, lasted only minutes in the intense firefight that ensued. Screams of terror mixed with the 'whump' and low singing whistle that came with newly fired mortar rounds and the whiz of AK-47s and M16s. Knowing that Company B's platoon leaders were inexperienced, Wright gave the company's forward artillery observer, 1st Lt. Fred G. Bragg, Jr., command of the company. Although Bragg had several months of combat experience, he radioed Wright, telling him that they had lost contact with the isolated platoon and were pinned down by enemy fire. Before Wright could do anything else to help, he had to return to Duc Co, fourteen miles away, to refuel his helicopter. "We had to hit the ground," Nat stated, "I mean, good God, when you get everything else shot at.... When I hit the ground there was a little dip there.... and I seen three or four hand grenades come in on me, but they never did go off.... But, you know, a lot of the hand grenades the Vietnamese had were duds."

Overhead, the fighter-bombers had arrived and were circling, awaiting the opportunity to strike. The FAC (Forward Air Controller) requested the artillery supporting Company B be shifted so the planes could come in and drop their ordnance. Bragg objected to this maneuver, but was countermanded by the 2nd Brigade, the headquarters controlling Wright's battalion, so a check fire was ordered on the artillery. The planes attacked, but with no discernible effect on the battle raging below, and Company B remained without artillery support for half an hour until Lt. Col. Wright returned and ordered them back into action, but it was too late. "It all happened so fast," Nat stated. "I had my radio shot off my back, guys were getting killed all around me. We called in the artillery fire, but it was hitting too far off.... Our FO (Forward Observer) only had two days left in-country, and the next thing I knew, he was killed, too. Then the CO....Captain Brian Rushton... I carried his radio. He was one of the first men to be killed. Hell, you couldn't keep him down," Nat said. "When we got the report from our first squad that they had three men down, he jumped up and said he was gonna go see what's going on. The next thing I knew he got hit with three rounds, with one hitting him right between the eyes. I had all his codes and everything on me 'cause he was new and wanted me to carry it all, even the damn maps!" I asked Nat why the CO would give all his critical information to his RTO, and Nat replied, "He said, 'You just keep this and let me get used to all this other.' They, hell..." Nat said and chuckled lightly.

"Our Battalion Commander was flying very high above us in a chopper. Hell, he was so high you could hardly even see him, but he said, 'It looks like you boys have everything under control. You got all the artillery and the air force with you....' We had it under control all right," Nat stated sarcastically. "I told him to go to hell.

Then I tried to call in an air strike, but we didn't have the right kind of smoke, so I told them to go to hell, too! There wasn't nothing else I *could* do! I was trying to use the radio our squad RTO had 'cause he was already dead. Hell, I couldn't call in the artillery, we didn't know how! I tried, though, and called it in anyway and told them to drop it in on top of us, but, hell.... It was hitting a way over yonder and not doing any good. Hell, all the officers were already dead, and what smoke we had was on dead bodies."

"Then that damn rocket come in.... I heard it a-coming, and that's the last I remember. It picked me up and threw me about thirty feet, I guess. Then I come to.... I was in a daze, though... My clothes was just threads, and the fatigues was split to the waist on both sides, and the shirt was, too, from the blast of the rocket. I don't know what kind of rocket it was, but it blew both my boots off. I got shrapnel in the right ankle from it."

When Nat awoke and realized what had happened, only five men had survived the vicious attack. Later, reports of the incident estimated the two companies had faced at least a battalion size force of the 66th North Vietnamese Regiment. One man of the 130-man Company C survived for two days after his capture, then he also died. Therefore, the entire Company perished in that battle. A total of 211 gallant men lay dead on the bloody jungle floor. As the only survivor of Company B, formerly eighty-five men strong, Nat and four others of the original-lead platoon had escaped with their lives. The four surviving men, however, now faced an even worse fear than death. Now they were Prisoners of War.

Chapter 4

Struggle to Adjust - Camp 101

"The next thing I remember was waking up about four hours later and realizing I had been tied to a bamboo pole with two female Dinks carrying me... or running... I don't know..." Nat paused. "After a while they stopped, untied me, and told me to walk. I had not walked very far until I saw four men that had been in the lead platoon, so they put us all together, but kept us far enough apart that we couldn't talk that much. Mac, Perricone, Newell, and Frank was in the first platoon we sent out and I lost contact with them on the radio when they moved out. They didn't know I was captured, and I didn't know they was captured, but then late that evening me and Perricone crossed paths when we were crossing a big stream. He was on one side, and I was on the other so we tried to holler at each other, and the Viet Cong started running off in unknown tongue for us to shut up!" Nat laughed. "And then I didn't see 'em until the next morning, and the others thought Perricone hadn't really seen me, and I was wondering the same thing, too."

"I was the 3rd Platoon's RTO, but then after all the rotations I was transferred to headquarters to be the RTO for the Old Man. The five of us, though, for five months was in the same platoon. I had been in headquarters for maybe a month and a half or two months. Lieutenant Hackett was the 3rd Platoon's Lieutenant when I was in it. Then he got rotated back, and I was sent up to headquarters as RTO. If it hadn't been for his rotating out, though, I would probably be dead right now 'cause it was that platoon that went out on the first patrol. Stanley Newell and I even went through basic and AIT at Fort Polk, then danged if we didn't get in the same outfit in Vietnam. That's really unusual."

"The first night we spent in [enemy] foxholes while U.S. planes dropped flares all night looking for us. There was also some artillery and air strikes. Hell, the whole side of the mountain was lit up, and some of the artillery hit pretty close... a lot closer than I liked, actually." I then asked Nat what his first night in captivity was like. "Well, they put us in foxholes in the side of this big mountain. Hell, it was bigger than that one over yonder," he stated and pointed to a huge, steep mountain that shadowed the home where he now lives. "I had a hammock in the foxhole, but couldn't stay in it because my hands and feet were tied, and we were all blindfolded... like you could see anything when it was dark. It was a long, lonely night and not very comfortable."

After a long, terrifying night filled with uncertainty, Nat was finally placed with the other men that had been captured the same time as him. All the prisoners were suffering from wounds received in battle, but had received no medical attention thus far. These other men included SSgt. Martin S. Frank of Belleville, New Jersey, E5/US Army. Frank had received a gunshot wound to his buttocks then exited through the front of his upper leg. He had difficulty sitting or even lying down without experiencing excruciating pain, and walking was difficult at best. The second man was SSgt. Richard R. Perricone of Uniondale, New York. Richard had been shot through the leg. SSgt. Stan Newell from Pekin, Illinois, had been shot in the shoulder, and was the third man of the other four prisoners to meet with Nat the first morning of their captivity. Two days later, these four would meet with Cordine McMurray, Sgt. First Class, from Detroit, Michigan. McMurray, the only black man in the group, had received a gunshot wound through the calf of his right leg.

"That morning we were given a rice ball to eat and told we would be taken to a POW camp." Nat and Martin Frank were tied together and blindfolded for the march through the jungle. "We walked for about five or six hours when we came to what they called a camp, but it was more like a military post or something. The officer I met there could speak better English than the one I had the first day. He wanted all kinds of answers, and I didn't know the answers," Nat said. "He [the interrogator] said I would have to cooperate, but our COC says name, rank, serial number, and date of birth." Is that all you gave him? "Yeah," Nat continued, "but that didn't go over very good. He told me the name of my company and the unit. He would interrogate us one at a time, but none of us told him much. He would say, 'You lie... You deceive... We're 'gonna kill you... We can shoot you.' I said, 'Hell, I was carrying these [codes], and the man's dead, and I'm not no officer.' Then he would say, 'Why you carry that?' and on and on.... Then after we got to the first camp they finally decided I wasn't an officer. I don't know what all kinds of codes I had, but... it was stuff he [Company Commander] used for the battalion, including locations and all, but, hell, I didn't know what they were. I never used them, he did. He had all his notes, too, 'cause he took notes everyday. I guess 'cause he was a new commander he didn't know any better and had been at headquarters all the time, but he wanted his CIB [Combat Infantry Badge]. He had never had to shave in the field with cold water and all, and he would cut himself every time he tried and bleed all over the place. Hell, the rest of us would just laugh and shake our heads. But he always kept all his stuff in a plastic envelope, but I never went through it. They [NVA] knew what they had 'cause they was intelligent, and a lot of times they would get on the same frequency as our radio, and they had certain codes, so he knew which frequency to switch to cause they were all written down. He [the interrogator] would ask me, 'Why you use all these?'.... Well, I just told him, 'Hell, I don't know... All I do is talk on it!'" We both laughed.

How did you end up being the RTO? "Well, I was trained as a rifleman, but then I started out as the RTO for the lieutenant in our platoon. The guys started rotating out, so they picked me to go to headquarters, which was supposed to be easy 'cause I stayed with the Old Man [HQ's Company Commander] all the time and didn't have to go out and pull perimeter guard at night. We stayed in the middle. I was a rifleman probably a month before I was made the RTO."

How was the trip getting to this first camp? "It was rough," Nat recalled. "'Cause, see, I didn't have no shoes. I was hit in the right ankle, and they tied me and Frank together, so the first day I walked with nothing but my socks on. Then they made Frank take off his left boot and give it to me so that way we both had one boot on." Did they give any explanation as to why they gave you each one boot? "They said I was a limping.... Well, my God, I was limping anyway with shrapnel in my ankle, but hell no, they give me one [boot] for *the other* foot! But I walked all the first day with just my socks on, and your feet's tender, you know, and.... I don't know which was worse, having one boot to wear or having nothing at all. The trail was muddy and full of snags and black, stinging ants. My feet bled for two days and was nothing but blisters and sores."

How was the terrain? "Well, it was getting a lot rougher, 'cause we was headed for Cambodia. We was right on the Cambodian border, anyway... It was rougher the first three or four days 'cause we was crossing that mountain. The U.S. hadn't been in that part yet with all their napalm and all... It hadn't been cleared out, so it was real rough," Nat replied. It's bad enough for soldiers trying to traverse the jungle terrain while wearing the tough, durable boots issued by the military, but crossing the same territory with socks or bare feet is almost incomprehensible. The jungle floor was covered with thick brush and rising fern with sharp, jabbing stakes left by crudely slashed undergrowth that pierced the tender flesh of the newly captured soldiers. Large broadleaf trees grew to encompass the middle height of the jungle canopy, while giant hardwoods rising to heights over 100 feet towered over all the other foliage. At each level, the huge trees interlocked their limbs to form a triple canopy that all but totally blocked out the bright tropical sun, thereby Casting a threatening darkness below. Within the arms of the jungle, dampness lingered, emitting the smell of rotting ferns and vines, while providing a lush breeding ground for leeches, poisonous spiders, and hordes of bloodthirsty mosquitoes.

"Then we run into the Montagnards. It was a tribe of people that lived way out and.... well, they were just... my God, the women and all... Most just wore a cloth or something, no blouse. It was about the third day or so, and we were going through a whole village of them, and this big old mamasan got after me with a damn pitchfork! I don't know what she done that for, but after we finally got to the camp where they could half-way speak English, one of 'em told me she did that because she probably had a son or daughter or something that had been killed by our military. Then we met two or three more, and they beat the hell out of you with a damn stick. I must have looked odd as hell or something, 'cause it was always me they attacked. We met several people on the trail... Some would just stare at us; others would hit and yell at us... probably cussing us."

Montagnards were tribes of mountain people, each with their own dialect and territory. Called "Moi" by the VC, meaning barbarian, the Vietnamese treated them with contempt, ridiculed them for their religious beliefs and customs, forbade them to speak their own language, and fined the tribesmen for wearing their loin cloths. Many years ago, they had been driven from China to settle mainly in the mountain ranges of Indochina. Steering clear of the lowland Vietnamese, who treated them with contempt and called them savages, the Montagnards moved high into the mountain regions. By utilizing the slash-and-burn method of agriculture, these hardy people would clear a small area in the thick jungle and grow corn, cassava, and yams for three to four years until the thin soil was depleted. At that time they would move on and start the process all over again. The Montagnards lived a communal life in thatch-roofed houses build on stilts. To return their hatred of those ridiculing them, the Montagnards fought willingly with American Green Berets and other Special Forces to kill the Vietnamese. Called "Yards" for short, the Montagnards developed "FULRO," an underground resistance group with a French meaning of "United Front for the Struggle of the Oppressed Races." These men were highly effective soldiers in their home territory and proved themselves to be loyal, brave, and deadly mercenaries. Very few Yards held resentment against the U.S. military, but for those who did and had the opportunity, American prisoners received vicious attacks.

A foreign correspondent, presumably French, rushed up to the POWs once somewhere along the trail and snapped a photograph of four of the five men as they were being moved to the prison camp. "We was on a rope," Nat explained. "Everybody was tied to the rope, but it looks like we were in a compound. It was somewhere on the trail from the time we were captured until we got to Camp 101. I don't really remember the actual photo being taken, 'cause when we stopped there was so many people that just run up and looked at us and talking in unknown tongue that he [the photographer] could have been in there, and we didn't know it. The photograph wasn't released until '69, though. I think after it was released, the National League of Families was the first to run the photo. After they received it, Major Pritchard came and showed it to Mother two years later. That was the first time since I disappeared that she knew I was alive."

How far do you think you traveled before you arrived at the first prison camp? "I'd say it wasn't over four or five miles, really... We was about five miles inside the Cambodian border, but the way we went, my God... It took five days, but the way we were all wounded that was as fast as we could go." The men received no medical treatment for their wounds during the first few days. Infection plagued them and pus oozed from their gaping injuries. They had no choice but to bear the pain and increasing fevers from the rotting flesh.

What was it like after you made it to the first camp? "Well, we finally arrived at our first camp. There was three huts in the camp, and it had a bamboo fence around it. The camp [already] had two POWs in it. They put the five of us in the same hut, which was nice... We could at least talk. That hut was about eight feet by twelve feet. We were really just in a big cage-- barely enough room for all of us to lay down on the 'bed' as they called it... It was made of bamboo. Then on the end of it, they had the stocks that were trees with a half-moon cut into them that they put our legs in of at night. We got a pair of black pajamas, a hammock-like thing, more like a heavy sheet, and they gave us our Ho Chi Minh sandals without the straps."

"The next morning, we were taken to the interrogation hut to meet the camp commander. He told us we had to obey all camp rules and bow to the guards every time we saw them when we were outside our huts." What happened during the interrogations? "Well, in the first camp they really didn't treat us all that bad... We all smoked, and they didn't have cigarettes... All they had was paper and tobacco. When they would interrogate us, they would lay one right out on the edge [of the desk], and you was dying to get it, and then the damn thing [NVA] wouldn't give it to you... But he would smoke one right after the other so you could smell it." Nat paused again before he continued talking. "The first few days... I mean, God Almighty.... It [the interrogation] was all day long. I guess the first week or two it was... We all thought... I mean, my God, you know, hell, how long we 'gonna have to go through all this. They interrogated me a lot on those damn codes I had. They just kept saying that I was an officer, but I kept telling them, 'Hell, I ain't nothing but a Spec 4,' and then it took an act of Congress to ever get it through their heads as to what that was! The first week we were interrogated everyday, then it slacked off to a couple times a week."

How did you adjust to living in the jungle and being a captive? "It was hard," recalled Nat, "but really the only way we adjusted was telling tales. We talked about naming candies, you know, like Almond Joy. We would sit there all day trying to think of a candy bar someone else didn't know. We talked about movies, too, that was going on back before we got captured and wondered what was going on and changing with them. Same thing with vehicles, we wondered what in the hell a '68 Chevrolet would look like," he said, laughing heartily. "I guess *Gone With the Wind* we went through at least a dozen times. Then sometimes we talked about the popular songs that were being sung then." Nat laughed again then said, "Ol' McMurray was always singing one of his favorite songs. It was 'Detroit City.'"

"We also had contests to see who could tell the biggest tales. Then we talked about Basic Training and AIT, and what happened after we got over there. Frank and McMurray, they went over as a unit. Frank was a big talker, anyway, so he would tell us all about coming over on the ship, and how they brought over the whole unit. He had a lot to tell about that." Nat laughed again, "He was one of those guys that could say it's raining today and could make a ten minute talk about how the sky looked. He was a big talker... him and McMurray, both. Mac was always talking about the gangs in Detroit, Michigan, and how he had a brother killed, too. But he could pass a lot of time by telling stories, and he was funny, a real comedian. Except when he was scared," Nat chuckled.

What were the living conditions like in this first camp? "The food we got wasn't good nor was there [ever] enough. We learned in a hurry to like rice because that was all we had. Most of the time there was bugs in it or rat droppings when you got to the bottom. Time passed slow at the beginning, but I got used to it. We were allowed outside for fifteen minutes twice a day to exercise. Course, all five of us had some type of wound. The other guys had been shot, but they were all clean wounds. I had shrapnel in my right ankle. They did try to keep the wounds halfway clean and washed them out with water. Then one morning, ten days after our capture, the camp commander came and said the doctor was going to fix our wounds, so they took us one at a time to an empty hut in our compound. The doctor was an old man... He said we must be tough like all Vietnamese. They didn't use nothing to numb around the wounds. They put a tote-sack over our heads... It hurt like hell, but the sooner it was over the better. Then the CO told us how good we were being treated and all the rest of his bull. It was like a broken record... You heard the same old stuff over and over again. They kept telling me I was a 'Nixon die-hard' or 'American Imperialist.' I was allowed to go to the latrine twice a day and could communicate some with the other two prisoners already in the camp."

When the freshly captured POWs arrived at their first jungle camp, two other service men were already being held within its confines. One man, from Vallejo, CA, W1/US Army, David W. Sooter, was an OH23 helicopter pilot who had been shot down February 17, 1967, and had suffered extensive injuries. His arm had been broken and, without proper treatment, had not healed correctly. He had also been burned badly at the time of the crash. Sooter had been in the camp for more than a year when the others arrived. The second man, PFC Joe Delong, of McMinville, Tennessee, had been shot in the leg and had been in the camp for four months.

"I don't guess I'd been there more than about two or three weeks before I had a seizure. You see, I got a concussion from that rocket blast, which caused the seizures. It scared the hell outta them [the NVA], you know. They didn't know what to do, and I didn't know nothing until the next morning when I woke up and saw my legs was in stocks... Hell, I didn't know what was going on... I thought 'How in the hell did I get into this?' Then McMurray told me. He said, 'Man you 'bout died last night. I didn't know what happened to you!'" During the seizure, Nat had tried to swallow his tongue. His friend and fellow prisoner, Perricone, had stuck his finger in Nat's mouth to try and keep him from choking to death on his own tongue. The next morning, Perricone teased Nat about almost biting his finger off during the ordeal. They were very concerned about Nat's physical condition, and yet were helpless to do anything

35

for him other than offer support. "The Vietnamese said, 'You got heart problems?' Hell... I thought I had a heart attack or something. We didn't know it had been a seizure until after I got home, 'cause nobody had ever seen someone have a seizure."

The POWs were in constant fear not knowing what might happen next. Deep within enemy territory, and at the mercy of their captors, the prisoners were exposed to all the dangers of the jungle, from weather to wild animals. "We hadn't been there too long... It was before we tried to escape... The damn tigers or lions got to circling the camp and got to squalling. We told old McMurray, 'Them damn things will be in here in a few minutes.' And, damn, it was hot.... He took that old green hammock thing they give us and covered up in it. He got to where he wouldn't take a bath, and my God! Then being under that blanket and all... Whew!" Nat laughed then continued the story. "McMurray wasn't able to go get a bath, though. He got down so bad that we could pick him up under the arms and carry him. He thought if he didn't eat, he might get released. He was sick, though. He was sick for at least six months, and we had to take care of him. They called him an "Afro American"... Good Lord, he would get mad at them for that. They [the NVA] would tell him, 'You got kinky hair.'" When asked what was McMurray's reaction to that, Nat laughed really hard, then said, "I better not say."

The months passed slowly, and all the while the men entertained the thought of escaping. All U.S. troops were taught to at least try to escape if they were made Prisoners of War. "There was a bamboo fence all around the camp, and during the day they left the gate open. We could see out of it, and it wasn't too bad 'cause we could all walk around during the day after the first few weeks. We was trying to get all the information we could from the two guys that were already there, you know, like what it was like, and what they would do to us. We got to talking and decided to plan an escape. We could hear choppers of a day and knew we weren't that far from the border. So we thought if we could get back across the border, then we would have it made."

By October 1, 1967, almost three months after their capture, the seven men agreed to devise an escape attempt. The plan was set with a date of November 6. "That chopper pilot said he knew the country... He flew over it quite a bit, and we was gonna let him lead us. We thought if we got out, we would run into a [U.S.] unit. How we did it was, we got an old guard we called 'Shit face.' He would come up and talk and talk and get real close to you. We decided we would have two guys outside.... Perricone and Delong. So they got him [the guard] out, and then they got over there and got to pointing to the ground, then the guard went over and got to looking down. Delong was gonna hold him, and Perricone was gonna hit him in the head with a rock. He thought he would just hit him with that rock, but, hell, the more Perricone hit, the louder he screamed. So they [the NVA] come from everywhere. Hell, the ground shook when all the Dinks came running. I didn't [even] make it out of the camp until I ran into the bayonet of an AK-47. Hell, I just turned around and walked back like I didn't even know what was going on. Perricone, Sooter, and Delong actually made it out of the camp. Sooter and Perricone were captured within a few minutes, but Delong was killed in the escape attempt."

What happened to the guard? "They said we made an invalid out of the guard," Nat replied. "So apparently he had brain damage, and he may have died, I don't know. We messed him up, though. He didn't have no hair left on his head. We kept hitting him on the side of the head until there was hair all over that rock. Hell, we wanted out of there!

"Life got rough after that day. We were put two to a hut. Sooter and Perricone got beat up pretty bad after they were returned to their huts. Well, we all did, really....but especially them. They put us together in the huts, me and Frank, Perricone and Sooter, and Newell and McMurray. They kept us in stocks twenty-four hours a day, seven days a week for six months and six days. We didn't get that much rice to eat, and everyone stayed hungry. We got one bowl of rice and a piece of rock salt each day. The rice we got was always black with rat droppings in it. I hate to say it, but I ate it... It was hard to separate it out. When a person is hungry, they can eat about anything. While I was in the jungle, I guess I ate about everything from rats to fish eyes. We all had diarrhea and dysentery.

"We were allowed to go to the latrine twice a day, but none at night. If we had to go any other time we just spread the bars on the bamboo and went through the bed. Sometimes they would let us clean it up the next day, but, if not, then the rats or something else would get it during the night. When they let us go to the latrine... Well, hell... Sometimes they didn't let us go at all.... But when they did, they had two guards on us at all times. Hell, they locked and loaded! Why, they scared me so bad, I was afraid one of them son of a bitches would kill me!" Trips to the latrine were almost a luxury, yet toilet paper was extremely rare. The prisoners would often use dried banana leaves or other broadleaf vegetation as a substitute for this much-needed commodity.

During their time in the stocks, the prisoners were allowed no exercise at all. When the guards passed the huts, they would beat the men's feet with sticks while still secured in the stocks. The bloody and bullet ridden fatigues that belonged to Joe Delong were hung in the center of the camp until they rotted away completely. The guards would tell the other prisoners everyday, 'You see what happened to him.' This grim reminder was very effective and worked heavily on the morale of the camp, with the men becoming more depressed as the days dragged on.

"That [first] Christmas was a low point for me," Nat recalled. "Everyone's morale was on the bottom, and we had spent over a month with both legs in stocks. I hate to hear Christmas carols to this day," Nat said quietly. "About two weeks before Christmas they would play carols just loud enough so I could barely hear them. This made it one of the saddest times, if not *the* saddest of all the years I spent in prison."

"On Christmas Day they gave us a good meal. We got some kind of meat, more rice than average, and a cigarette to smoke after the meal. The only food we had had was rice and rock salt, so the good meal we got gave all [of us] diarrhea. The guards had a big laugh about it. The treatment we got didn't change and neither did the food. We were back on rice and rock salt the next day, and were put back into stocks again twenty-four hours a day."

Chapter 5

Camp 102

It was nothing short of hell on earth for the men in captivity. Morale was non-existent, the days passed like long, painful years, and now their friend Delong was dead. How much worse could it get? Not only did survival and living conditions grow worse, but little did these men know that the future would hold horrors they would relive time after time in the years to come. Hellish nightmares would rip out their guts and haunt the soul of even the most hardened veterans.

In February of 1968, the remaining six prisoners were moved to their second camp in the jungle. The trip was no more than a mile and a half from the first location, but it took over half a day to make the journey. Having been confined to stocks for so long, the men were extremely weak and in poor physical condition. Nat had developed beriberi that caused his legs and feet to swell until walking was almost impossible. Camp 102, as the prisoners named their second location, was very similar to the first. The layout was basically the same, only a little larger in size, but the entire camp was surrounded by pits of pungi stakes. "The pungi stakes were made out of bamboo. They were about one inch thick and sharpened on each end... They were very sharp," Nat recalled. "A lot of times they dipped one end in human waste, so when one of these stakes stuck you, the spot would become very infected and made a bad sore. I fell on two, and you can still see the scars there on my leg and arm."

"When they took us to the second camp, they had pungi stakes everywhere. They had 'em in every different direction, even going to the latrine. You had a real small path about that wide, [Nat indicated a space of eighteen inches], and you better walk it right. Old McMurray, he passed out there one time coming back from the latrine. He was just lucky 'cause he got almost back to the door of the hut... My God, if he'd a-fell before that, he would of had 'em from one end to the other."

"I fell on one going to the bath area and still have a scar on my arm. We didn't have nowhere to take a bath without going down a steep hill to a creek or branch. It was just as we were going out of the camp and through the dern gate. We had been in the stocks for so long and all that I had a stumbling attack or something and fell and hit my arm. I don't think it had anything on it, but the ones they put right inside the camp, they, hell, you could look at it and tell they was poisoned. I was always afraid I would fall on one and be stuck in the head, face, or stomach."

Once the prisoners arrived, "We went right back into stocks," Nat said. "The treatment didn't change at all. After we tried to escape from Camp 101, we were told that when the war was over, we would not be released, but held and tried as war criminals. We stayed in stocks until the first of May. Then it just so happened some high-ranking officer with the NVA happened to come by one day... He saw what [bad] shape all the POWs was in... We had beriberi so bad that we couldn't even move our ankles in the stocks 'cause they had swollen so bad... He made 'em let us out of the stocks during the day, but at night they put us right back in 'em. They wouldn't let us outside our huts, though. I was allowed outside some of the day for exercise sometimes later on. In this camp I did get a bath about once a week, where as in Camp 101 we probably never got a dozen baths the whole time I was there. They gave us soap, and once in a while tobacco in this camp, though... We rolled our own cigarettes and used paper from U.S. propaganda [leaflets] to wrap it in."

Did your food get better also? "We started getting soup with the rice then. If the POWs had stayed under those conditions, we probably would have all died. I will never forget the first meat we got... It was gibbon (monkey), but it was really good. Sometimes we also got manioc and bamboo shoots. I haven't eaten pumpkin pie since I came home, because we got that damned old punkin' soup when it was in [season]. We would get it every day for days on end. The only thing we got was the seeds and insides, the part you throw away. Hell, it must have stayed in season for two months 'cause that's all we got... that and a bowl of rice full of rat droppings. I wouldn't eat a punkin' pie to this day... There ain't no way! It ain't even allowed in this house!"

"The worst damn soup we got in the jungle was.... Well, I don't know what it was, but it had fish eyes in it. There was some things you just couldn't stand, but you could eat it or anything else to keep from starving to death. That was one of the hardest things I think I ever tried to eat! It didn't have no flavor, and it looked just like grease, and then you had them damn eyeballs floating in it. We teased McMurray and told him it had fins and other stuff in it... Course, it probably did for all we knew." Nat laughed, remembering McMurray's reactions to the soup. "We didn't have it too much, but we usually had it around September during their fishing season. The Vietnamese ate the fish, and we got the leftovers." Nat cringed slightly then continued. "You'd see that damned old big eye and, whew! That was the hardest thing I ever tried to eat. Hell, sometimes I got a bowl with two or three eyes in it, but one was more than enough!"

"I know one time there was a damn banana viper got up in the leaves in the hut next to mine. The banana viper was velvet green in color. They [the NVA] got all of the prisoners out of there, then the dang guards finally caught him and said they was gonna eat him. But the banana viper... They said if you got bit by it, then you better get to medical attention and quick. It was about like the one they called the "three-stepper." It was one kind of the cobra... I don't know if we ever got snake to eat, but a couple times we got some meat that we didn't know what was." Nat laughed, "I remember McMurray... There was an eyeball of some kind in the soup that same night, and he said he wasn't eating that thing... We all laughed, but he ended up eating every bit of it."

"Then we got some kind of bird in the jungle. It was a black bird... I don't reckon we got it over three or four times, though... There wasn't enough meat on it to feed us, so they put it in our soup.

41

The damn bones was all they was in it. We also got something that looked like these old water lilies. I don't know what it was. It was some kind of old greens, and it was tough! And then after the escape, that and rock salt was about all we got." Nat stopped and thought for a minute. "There was some kind of green pea, too. It looked a lot like black-eyed peas, which was fairly good. I know there was many, many times we would sit and say how good it would be to have the scraps off of somebody's dinner table... But we tried not to think of that because the more I thought, the hungrier I got. I said a lot of prayers while in the jungle."

"I guess the best thing we got in the jungle was bamboo shoots. Oh, God, I loved 'em!" Nat exclaimed. "When we got bamboo shoots they had to boil them twice, 'cause the first time you could get poisoned from it, so they always boiled them twice. I remember Benge telling us they had to be boiled twice. He also told me about one of the nurses he was captured with had gotten so bad she couldn't walk, and Benge told the NVA just to let them die. They told him no, that they would feed them good and give them better care, so they boiled the bamboo shoots just one time, and the damn things poisoned them. They damn near all died, the nurse actually did. But there wasn't no better eatin' than bamboo shoots."

"Michael Benge was captured right before the Tet of '68 with two nurses. He was a civilian that worked with the Montagnards trying to show them how to grow more vegetables and all. He was something like an agricultural agent. He had been over there a while, I think it was his second time over there, then after we got released he went back over there again and eventually married a Vietnamese."

Remembering one of the lighter times in the jungle, Nat related this next incident. "I remember a lot of times during the night we would have rats run across our feet while we were in the stocks. Sometimes I could feel something crossing, and if it took two or three minutes to cross, I knew then that it was a snake. One funny thing, I guess, about being in the jungle, when them snakes went across my legs at night, we told Ol' McMurray they was a-coming, and he had done turned white by the time they got to him!" Nat laughed hard remembering everyone teasing McMurray so bad, but then the next laugh was on him. "It was right after we had killed that damn banana viper. I don't guess it was over two or three days later that they put us in the stocks that night. It had just got good and dark and something hit my mosquito net and it bent it down to where I couldn't even sit up. It was like a damn turtle or something. Newell was next to me and he hollered to the guard 'bao cao', 'bao cao!' They come down, and we thought it was a big snake on my net at first. They come in there with a stick and flipped it outside. It left I reckon, and we never did figure out exactly what it was, but it was something like a turtle. You talk about a funny feeling," he said. "Them old mosquito nets wasn't much good anyhow, and here this thing come. It came down through the roof, which was made out of big, old, wide leaves like a palm or something. Hell, if that thing had got to me, somebody would have had skinned ankles 'cause I'd a-come outta there! Talk about walking on water, my God, I would'a walked on air to get away from that thing!"

From the damp of the jungle and atrocious food given to the prisoners, sores and oozing boils covered the men's flesh. The sores would start out small, then over time grow to be huge infected boils that produced feverish skin filled with water, blood, and pus. Unable to reach the boils on their backs, the prisoners would take turns with each other helping to relieve the painful sores. "I still have scars on my back from the boils," Nat said. "Some of them would get really big, and we didn't have any medicine to put on them. After getting to the north though, the boils went away."

At times life seemed a little more tolerable in Camp 102. The prisoners had begun to accept their fate and were able to adjust to their surroundings despite mal-nutrition, low morale, and endless interrogation sessions. Summer was approaching, and the men were released from stocks during the day, although the dread of night brought their swollen ankles back to the misery of confinement.

As the fighting in Vietnam escalated, more prisoners were brought into Camp 102. The men were not allowed to communicate verbally, but developed a sign language of their own to keep morale up and remain abreast of what was happening with others in the camp. "In the summer and fall of 1968," Nat recalled, "we had five or six new guys come into the camp. My morale and the other guys all got better. We shared the camp with Tom Horio, Leonard Daughtery, Gail Kerns, Peter Drabic, Stephen Leopold, Don McFail,

Mike Benge, Billy Smith, Jose Jacques, and Robert Zebulan. Mike Benge spoke fluent Vietnamese and was the only civilian prisoner. He would listen to what the guards was saying and could tell us what was going to happen most of the time."

"Life went better here since there was a few more guys in camp. We weren't allowed out in the courtyard with others. You were allowed out with men in your own cage only, but we still could talk to the other men from cage to cage because they were fairly close together. The only news I heard was when a new man was captured and brought to our camp. We all would ask the new guys a world of questions. Everything from movies, songs, what cars looked like, and even about the clothes that were in style. They [the NVA] would play Hanoi Hannah every so often. It was all propaganda, though. We would hear about all the planes that had been shot down and how many POWs were taken."

"When I was in this camp, the camp commander gave us some paper to make us a deck of cards," Nat stated. What did you have to make them out of, and what did you use to write on them? "Propaganda papers," he replied. "See, it was only written on on one side, so you could turn them over and use the back of it. They gave us a pen to write 'em with, then they took the pen back. The cards was about 1 ½. by 1 ½ inches in size, and it was hard to play with, but it did pass the time. This was after we were taken out of the stocks during the day." Why did they let you have them? "They told us that was a sign of the lenient treatment the Vietnamese was giving us. We kept them maybe two weeks, then they took them away from us again. They said our attitude was bad." Nat laughed, as he was always being told he had a bad attitude.

"I remember one time," Nat said, as he started to laugh again. "Frank, I don't know if he tore it off the pants leg of the pajamas or what, but he braided a little strip of cloth about six inches long one night. The guards had given us a cigarette to smoke before supper. They wouldn't let us smoke it after dinner, so when they came and gave us a light, we only smoked a puff or two, then we lit that braided cloth so we could smoke after supper." Nat started laughing again. "We put that cloth over in the backside of the hut so we could smoke our cigarettes when we got through eating. So when we got through, there was about two inches left of it still burning, then somebody lit a cigarette and we were all gonna get a light off of his, then here come the damn guards. They seen that and seen we hadn't smoked but a little of our cigarettes, so they took the cigarettes we had. Well, we didn't get no cigarettes that night!" Nat roared with laughter. "We never did that no more! When they gave us tobacco... Well, sometimes we would go four or five weeks without any, but then they'd give us a little bit." The laughter started again as he finished the story. "My God, you talk about strong! Hell, we'd get dizzy, you know, not smoking one for that long. It was like smoking the tobacco they raise around here [Western North Carolina]. It would take your breath and make you cough, and everything else!"

What was the monsoon season like in the jungle? "My God, it was like it rained for forty days and nights," Nat laughed, "and we didn't have no ark, either! Hell, it thundered and lightened over there the worst I've ever seen. They, my God, it lightened that whole damn jungle up. I was on the end of our bamboo bed and afraid I was gonna get hit. That thunder and lightening, though, would shake the ground over there," he stated, while a nervous laugh followed the words. "It was around the last of July and all of August, I think, and there was days that we would get up of a morning and eat the rice, then lay down and sleep all day. It would rain all day and all night, too. Conditions didn't really get worse, but everything stayed damp and cold. My God, it was cold! When it wasn't raining, though, the sky over there was the bluest sky I've ever seen. Some of my hardest times in the jungle was during the summers. The sky was so blue that it reminded me of fall here in the mountains of North Carolina. It would make you homesick as hell."

The death of a fellow prisoner was always the hardest reality for the men to face and accept. Starvation, disease, extreme tortures, and animals from the jungle all took their share of life from the men in captivity. "We had a guy die in our Camp in '69. He said his name was Robert Zeb. He had been captured in September 1966 and had spent most of his time in solitary. His mind had really gotten bad... Robert was very weak with malaria, and we would go down [to his hut] at night and put the mosquito net on him... Hell, I was afraid of him," Nat stated. "His eyes were dancing and he didn't have the strength to get up, but it was still scary."

"I remember about two months before this incident, he screamed

45

at one of the guards. 'You son-of-a-bitch! If I could ever get your fucking ass in the United States, I would put you in a damn cage and make you drink carrot juice!' He was upset over our food. We had some really bad stuff to eat. I think that day we had had fish soup with a couple of eyes in the soup. We had to eat what they gave us or starve to death, but that fish soup was the hardest thing we had to eat."

"The camp commander came down one day when Zeb was really sick and took Stan Newell and myself to the interrogation hut and told us we were to give Zeb blood, which we did. We didn't care 'cause we wanted to help him get his strength back. They finally got our blood and gave him the transfusion, but he died later that night. They never checked our blood types... Our blood may not have matched with his. He died around 10:00 that night and was still in solitary confinement when he died. They took the body out of the camp. We never saw the body, but we were positive that he had died. The next day the camp commander came and told us he was dead."

Chapter 6

Hearts at Home

While the fate of Sergeant Henry remained a mystery, his parents back in the States were trying to cope with the capture of their youngest son. Conditions at home were nearly intolerable. "It was just me and Thurman here," Mrs. Henry commented. During our interview I asked Mrs. Henry how long Nat had been gone before she found out he was missing. "I got a letter from him on Wednesday, July 12, 1967," she replied, "and that was the day he was captured. Then they [the Army Officials] came on the 15th and told us he was missing." A pause in her response revealed that she was remembering one of the most horrible days of her life. After a few hard swallows Mrs. Henry continued. "I thought...... Well, it was terrible," she said through the choking tears. "They were sending out flyers and all trying to find him, but they couldn't."

How long was it before you realized he was still alive and a Prisoner of War? A long silence hung in the air of the small country kitchen as we sat at the table where thousands of home-cooked meals had crossed its surface. The kind and gentle face of Mrs. Henry changed abruptly with the painful memories that now flooded her mind. Years of fear and uncertainty flushed from deep within their silent tomb and spilled onto her cheeks in soft, rolling tears. After almost thirty years later, a mother's pain was still as fresh and deep as it had been the day she got the unthinkable news that her youngest son had disappeared. A verbal response barely escaped the constricted throat of this loving mother, while the pain in her face spoke more words than could ever be written. The only reply she could give was, "I refused to believe it."

What did you do to keep your strength up? "I worked all the time," she said. "My husband didn't do anything for ten months. After that ten months, though, he went to work for Mr. Wilson over here building that ranch-style house down there below the church. Then a year later after Harry got home, him and Harry built the Burningtown Lakes and all the houses over there. Thurman was just so tore up at first that he couldn't work, so he just decided to stay home. At the time he couldn't take anything like that. It was hard on him. But, really..... Women just have to be the rock of the family." Her words barely choked out before another flood of tears washed her face with painful lines. Reaching over, I gently squeezed her hand for reassurance, and she held mine while trying to regain her composure. The memories were still vivid in her mind, and the pain was tearing at her heart. "I always just block everything out of my mind," she replied through the tears. We both wiped our eyes and tried to make light of a situation that hung heavy in the air. The beginning of a beautiful spring day allowed bright rays of sunshine to filter through the windows and splash upon the table before us. The glorious rays of freedom brought renewed strength and affirmation that hope and faith exists even in the most trying of times.

"We had a contact officer that came every month to keep us up to date about everything that was going on," Mrs. Henry said in a soft voice. "We always looked forward to his visits. It helped a lot. We had two, really.... One got transferred, and they brought in another one later on. Major Tucker was the first one, and Major Charlie Pritchard was the second one. Furman McGaha was killed [in Vietnam] and got brought back about 1967, I guess, and Major Tucker was the one that brought him back here to be buried. Major Tucker was then assigned as our contact officer, and he called and talked to everybody about us. He was finding out from everybody else besides me what was going on! I don't know why that made me so mad, but I wrote this man in Washington and told him just what I thought about it, and, you know, he called Major Tucker. He [Tucker] was stationed in Georgia, and the Department of the Army in Washington said, 'Now you go right now and [talk to Mrs.

Henry] and don't you stop for a minute!" Mrs. Henry laughed at the response her letter had provoked from the Washington official to Major Tucker. "Well, then after Major Tucker come up here, he said, 'You know, I don't know what you're doing, but you just about caused me to lose my rank!' I said, 'I just wrote a letter.' He always laughed about that and said, 'Just let you get a hold of a letter to write [in the future] 'cause you can sure get things done!'" Laughter erupted again as Mrs. Henry recalled the Major's response. "Well, that taught him a lesson! After that he came every month to tell me if there was a meeting or anything going on."

"That man in Washington, he was the head of the Army. I don't remember his name right now, but I could write to him about anything and he would see to it that it got done," continued Mrs. Henry. "I know when Harry was in Cam Ranh Bay, I sent him an address and told him he could write and get in touch [with Nat] that way. But then Harry took the letter and went to his commanding officer, but the officer replied and said, 'Don't you write! You write back to your mother and tell her not to be writing to that address.' They [the U.S.] didn't want them [the NVA] to know that we knew they had somebody. It was all confidential, so I didn't write no more."

The Department of the Army kept in close, constant contact with the Henry family regarding the status of their son, Nat. Major General Kenneth G. Wickham, the Adjutant General at that time, sent numerous letters and documents pertaining to American servicemen listed as POWs or MIAs to the Henrys. Mrs. Henry had kept the majority of correspondence generated from that and numerous other organizations, which upon inspection almost thirty years later provided invaluable information and insight into the political realm during the height of the Vietnam War. Each letter addressed to the Henrys from Major General Wickham began exactly the same: *"I am writing you concerning your son, Specialist Four Nathan B. Henry, who has been a prisoner in Vietnam since July 1967."*

To see those same words on hundreds of documents, year after year, seemed cold and devoid of any concern. Form letters from the government, followed by volumes of pages containing an overwhelming conveyance of, "Sorry, but there is little we can do," provided only slight comfort to the family. In reality, the more

49

correspondence the Henry family received, the more frustrating it became trying to interpret the underlying messages contained in the pages. After the first few years, Thurman, Nat's father, simply quit reading the letters and depended upon his wife to read and sort through the mounds of near useless paper.

It was very difficult for members of the Henry family to know that Nat was being held prisoner somewhere in Vietnam, yet were unable to communicate with him even through letters. Political pressures and an ever-increasing uncertainty as to the fate of the POWs simply made the situation unbearable for the folks at home. There's no way of knowing whether the address the Henry's had concerning Nat's location was valid, or whether their letters would ever have been delivered to his hands. But with the restrictions imposed on them by the Department of the Army, a situation in which they could do little more than hope had just grown more frustrating and rendered them even more helpless than before.

"The Army never found out that he was alive until January of '73," said Mrs. Henry. "That was the first time that *they* knew he was alive. Two years, though, after he had been captured, we got this picture. It showed four of them being guarded by a Vietnamese." So that confirmed to you that he was still alive? "Well, that's what I told Major Tucker when he brought it. I identified one of the boys with him because his mother had sent me his picture. I had never seen him, but I told Major Tucker that that was Stanley Newell, so they knew. I told him which one was Nat and which one was Stanley, but I didn't know the other two. Later we found out that one was Martin Frank, and Richard Perricone was the other one. I didn't know Perricone, but I knew his mother 'cause we had been writing to each other, but I didn't know it was her son. Then later Major Tucker called me back and said that his [Newell's] mother had identified him, too. We got in touch with each other through the American League of Families. We agreed to let them release our names, so that's how I ended up getting in touch with her."

"That picture wasn't nothing to prove that he was living, but, you know.... You knew in your heart that he was still alive, and I told him [Major Tucker] that. He said he may have to come, and it might be midnight or 2 o'clock in the morning, but whenever they have this meeting to decide whether he [Nat] was still living or not,

50

he would come tell us. Then I said, 'Well, you can come and tell me, and you can even bring a body back here, and we'll bury it, but it still won't be him, 'cause I knew he wasn't dead," Mrs. Henry stated. "Then Major Tucker said, 'Well, as long as *you* feel that way, then *I* feel that way!'"

On Friday, May 16, 1969, Major Tucker visited the family with a photograph snapped by a French news correspondent. Depicted in the black and white snapshot were four American servicemen being held by an armed Viet Cong "somewhere" in the jungles of Vietnam. Years later, our discussion of the matter revealed the photograph was taken somewhere on the trail to Camp 101 shortly after Nat's capture occurred. "The picture was probably taken on the trail," Nat later remarked, "because I could tell we still had fresh wounds." It was not, however, until the Henry family positively identified their son in the photograph two years later that the Army changed Nat's status from Missing in Action to Prisoner of War.

"I argued with them all the time," she continued, referring to the Army officials in Washington. "I said, 'He's in Cambodia,' but they said, 'No, he's not in Cambodia,' but he was. They didn't think they [the NVA] took any prisoners through Cambodia. But there was this one boy; he was there after the battle. He didn't tell me until after Nat come home, but he said, 'I couldn't come tell you that I looked all over the place where the battle had been checking the bodies looking for him.' They thought for sure he had been killed. He was one of the boys that was over there with him. Nat wrote [earlier] and said that this boy would get in touch with me when he come home, but when he come home we already knew that Nat was missing. He said he went through all that area where the battle was at, and that he didn't think it was possible for anybody to have lived through it. He and Nat had met over there, and his buddy had searched the battle zone. His name was Eddie Moody, and he was from over in Waynesville. I even got letters from some of the officers."

"There was another boy, Toby Hughes. He was one of the boys that always went camping with Nat. He came back [from Vietnam] one day, it was a Sunday, and he stopped out there in the yard. He was just standing there, and I just went running down the steps and grabbed him, and I said, 'You get in here!' After he come in [the house] he said, 'I'd never have been able to move if you hadn't come out there.' He said, 'I went in a plane over that battlefield, and I couldn't imagine he was still alive.' I don't know if he and Nat met over there, but you know how they always know about each other."

"Major Tucker came over one time and I said, 'Nat's name's not on the list of the dead.' He said, 'Well how in the world do you know that?' I just showed him a piece of paper I had and said, 'Are you gonna tell this?' And he replied, 'Why, no, I'm not gonna tell nothing,' and so he read it over. Then he asked how in the world did I get a list of the dead? I told him that a friend of a friend that was working in that [Army] department had sent us a copy. Major Tucker then said, 'I'll swear, you can pull more strings than anybody I know!'" Mrs. Henry laughed, "Then I said, 'Don't you dare tell that,' and he said he wouldn't. Well, we sat there for a few minutes, and then he said, 'You know, if that had been me, I'd a done the same thing."

"He was really a good man, though," Mrs. Henry commented. "I told him he was an Army brat 'cause he had been in the service all his life. He just laughed and said, 'Well, you just tell it like it is!' When he brought Major Pritchard to meet us, he laughed and said, 'Y'all get along just like people who have always known each other,'" Mrs. Henry said through a hearty laugh. "He said that 'cause Major Pritchard asked me if I had ever fixed poke salad and all that, and I said, 'Well, yeah!" she exclaimed, laughing again while remembering the conversation. "But I could call them any time if I needed anything. If they needed to get in touch with me, they would even call me when I was working at Beldens." [Beldens was a local manufacturing plant at that time.]

What was happening with your other two sons during this time? "Well, Pratt wasn't overseas, but Harry was in Cam Ranh Bay, and, well, I'd send Harry packages, too," she stated. "Course he had it easy where he was at. I don't know why they did it, but they gave him officer's quarters, and he had everything nice there. Musta been [that way] because his brother was a POW. He was a construction engineer, and they was building a dock or something over there. Harry left a month after Nat was captured. When he left, though, he said he was gonna kill two of them for every one of ours. They bombed around where he was at, but he didn't see any combat."

"I remember Major Pritchard come up here one evening late, and he said, 'Oh, I'm gonna have Harry transferred somewhere else.' But when Harry got the word, he sent word back that he wasn't *being* transferred! He ended up staying a year in Cam Ranh Bay. They wanted to transfer him to Hawaii or somewhere, but he didn't want to go. He wanted to stay there 'cause he was used to everything," Mrs. Henry paused a moment then remembered a strange incident that happened to her son, Harry. "A funny thing happened one night as him and his buddy was sitting around talking. His buddy was going through some of his things, and he showed Harry a picture and said, 'Look there, wasn't that a terrible wreck?' Harry looked at that picture and said, 'Well I was the one that was in it!' They was both shocked, and after all that time, too. His buddy was from Ohio and was a cub reporter in Georgia at that time and had taken that picture. Whenever he started to leave and when Harry was coming home, he gave Harry that picture. It really is a small world." The picture was from the wreck Harry was in during his stay at Fort Gordon, Georgia.

Harry Henry refused a reassignment from his post in Cam Rhon Bay. In a letter home dated March 19, 1968, Harry stated that the Department of the Army had notified him that he had been reclassified as the sole surviving son and could request a reassignment. Without knowing where he would be sent, Harry decided to stay in Cam Rhon Bay and request an early out. On June 3, 1968, Harry left Vietnam headed for Fort Lewis, Washington. By August 13 of the same year, he was back home with his family to offer support and continue to wait for several years to come before his younger brother would return home and make the family whole once again.

How about people from town? Did anyone help you out or do special favors for you while Nat was in captivity? "Zeb Meadows was the postmaster at that time, and he would send me a big box of letters that had come in. They were from every state in the union except Alaska. Alaska, I think, was the only one I didn't hear from. There was just people from everywhere that wrote just to see if there was anything they could do. We kept getting letters right up until the time he was released."

"Mr. Meadows sent the packages [to Nat] for me, even though he knew they would come back, but we sent them everywhere. We sent them to Moscow and every country over there hoping they would forward them on. We was hoping they would be, but they wasn't. He and Catherine Deal, they were both *so* good. I know one time he called me, and I had to go get the package 'cause it was one ounce over. He said, 'I would have opened it, but I didn't know what to take out!' I said, 'Well, you could have took out anything, and it would have been all right." Mrs. Henry laughed. "But he was real good about everything. We kept sending Nat packages, though. Sometimes it would take eighteen months for them to come back, but Mr. Meadows would always put something on it that they had to come back. He said that way we'll know if he gets them or not. They [the NVA] had been through them, too, with a fine-toothed comb. I had sent him a bunch of bouillon cubes and wrote him a little note to dissolve them in water and drink them. I had put them down in the bottom of the package, but they had taken them out. They just throw'd it all back together, 'cause everything was all messed up when they came back."

"Vic Perry [a local druggist] would give me little packs of sugar to put in the package, too. He said we could put in so many of those, and they would stay fresh. He was awful good, too. I remember Jack Dillard [manager] from the A&P store would order me canned hams. They were from Denmark, I think. They didn't have to be refrigerated, you know. I would always put one of those in, but they come back. too. I felt terrible when that happened, but Mr. Dillard was awful good to order me the hams. They didn't usually sell that many of them, but he always had one ordered for me."

"Let me find my Bible," Mrs. Henry said, as she rose from her chair. "I might still have a list in it of things we could send. That will just give you an idea." Mrs. Henry came back to the table carrying a large white family Bible. Flipping through the pages, she found the package tag and showed it to me. "I don't know why I kept that, but I did," she said. The following list details the contents and cost of one of the many packages Mrs. Henry sent to Vietnam while Nat was captured:

- 1 canned ham $2.35
- 1 fruit cake   1.79
- 1 toothache kit   .79
- 1 toothbrush   .39
- 1 toothpaste   .89

- 1 deodorant spray   .79
- 1 Kool-Aid   .25
- 1 soap   .25
- 1 medicated powder
- 2 pkg. Cigarettes   .50
- 2 bouillon cubes   .39
- 1 hard candy   .39

Total value of the package was $8.06. (No value was listed for the medicated powder). This particular tag was attached to the package that contained the listed items above and sent to Col. Hal Ba Trung – Hanoi Democratic Republic – Vietnam, by way of Moscow, USSR, on December 11, 1970. Like the dozens of packages before, this too was returned to the Henry family with certain items removed by the NVA. During the entire time of captivity, nothing the Henry family sent ever reached their son Nat in the prison camps of Hanoi.

Chapter 7

Dragons Against Ho

Ho Chi Minh. Born in 1892 and given the name of Nguyen Tat Thanh in 1902, Ho left Vietnam for France in 1917 to embark upon a revolutionary career. Minh was a determined man with a well-conceived plan-- a nationalist revolutionary dedicated to the expansion of communism in Indochina. Ho was a member of the French Communist party, the Russian Community party, founder of the Indochinese Communist Party (ICP), the Viet Minh League, and the Lao Dong party. Ho designed a successful communist revolution and was head of a communist state, while holding two leading Western powers at bay-- France and Japan. Minh's doctrine was Marxism. That explained the world and how it operated, while his method, Stalinism, taught him how to use, then eliminate, allies. Ho Chi Minh spent twenty-five years working tirelessly for the international communist movement. During this time he suffered severe privations, served time in prison, and mastered the technique of survival.

On August 28, 1942, Ho Chi Minh, disguised as a blind Nung and then later a Chinese journalist, entered China to offer the Kuomintang the intelligence service of the Viet Minh in exchange for Chinese military aid to support his revolutionary movement in Vietnam. Thinking the Kuomintang would favor his intelligence information on Japanese troop movements in Indochina, Ho decided to negotiate this intricate deal himself. In contrast to his thinking, however, the Kuomintang had broken with the communists and looked unfavorably upon the activities of the Viet Minh in both China and Vietnam. The Kuomintang coldly rejected Ho's offer, and, subsequently, General Chiang Fa-ku'ei, the military governor of Kwangsi (China), ordered the ICP leader to be imprisoned on charges of being a French spy.

Kept several months in a revoltingly primitive Chinese jail, Ho was placed under temporary house arrest, then moved to various places in Luichow and Kweilin. "It was at Kweilin that my teeth began to fall out," Ho stated years later. "I looked at myself once and tried never to look again. I was skin and bones and covered with rotten sores. I guess I was pretty sick."

Ho was kept in prison for a little over a year. During this time he wrote classical Chinese poetry and philosophical phrases depicting his thoughts. Describing this time he said, "Using my tears for ink, I turn my thoughts into verses." Looking at the leg irons that securely locked him to the floor at night he wrote:

With hungry mouth open like a wicked monster
Each night the irons devour the legs of people:
The jaws grip the right leg of every prisoner:
Only the left is free to bend and stretch.

Referencing himself as a professional agitator, Ho had not felt safe anywhere except in jail and wrote accordingly:

Yet there is one thing stranger in this world:
People rush in to place their legs in irons.
Once they are shackled, they can sleep in peace.
Otherwise, they would have no place to lay their heads.

Ho strongly believed that misfortune tested men and that the prisoners of today would be the rulers of tomorrow:

People who come out of prison can build up a country.
Misfortune is a test of people's fidelity.
Those who protest at injustice are people of true merit.
When the prison doors are opened, the real dragon will fly out.

Ho Chi Minh was released from the Chinese prison on September 16, 1943. Two years later, on September 2, 1945, he became president of the Democratic Republic of Vietnam. Did Ho Chi Minh know something others didn't about power and control? In this writer's opinion, the above verses taken from Ho's prison diary depict just that. Having served time himself in a foreign prison, did Ho really believe that "when the prison doors are opened, the real dragon will fly out?" My own interpretation of his writings substantiates the severe and inhumane treatment of our men during his rule. Maintaining our men in the most severe guttural conditions gave Ho, in his rationale, an upper hand on the most deadly dragon of all. Learning only fear and hate from his own imprisonment, Ho would more expectantly have learned from his own reactions to this cruelty, in that his treatment of the "dragon" he was confronting (U.S. Forces) would only serve as the Biblical plagues did to Pharaoh- - they only hardened the dragon's heart.

The spirits of our men could not be beaten, though. The more they protested the injustice of the Vietnamese prison system, which didn't acknowledge the Geneva Convention, the more their treatment centered on total repression. Yet despite the wretched treatment our prisoners received, their spirits and loyalty to the Code and to each other could not be broken. Did their refusal to compromise their belief in the Code send a strong message to Ho, exposing to him the most sincere merit of all? And why, after Ho Chi Minh died, did the tortures and beatings begin to ease up, while rations of food slowly improved? A coincidence? I think not.

Nat recalled the day Ho Chi Minh passed on to another world. "Ho Chi Minh died on September 3, 1969. We didn't know what in the hell was going on. The guards all went into mourning and all wore black armbands. I didn't know if our treatment would get better or worse, but our treatment didn't change in the jungle. A month later, Frank and I were called to the interrogation hut. The camp commander asked us what had happened on September 3, and Frank said, 'Oh, that was Ho Chi Croak Day.' That really went over!" Nat said with a regretful chuckle. "The guard took us back to the hut, and we stayed inside without getting to go to exercise any during the day." Minh's death, along with public awareness from the August '69 early release of Douglas Hegdahl, Robert Frishman, and Wesley Rumble, and their accounting of the treatment inflicted upon American POWs, forced the North Vietnamese to ease up on their torture sessions. Although the torture was less severe, it certainly didn't end.

May 19, 1969, then Secretary of Defense Melvin Laird appealed to Hanoi to release the lists of American prisoners. The request fell on deaf ears, and once again North Vietnam stated no information would be released concerning our prisoners until the U.S. agreed to full troop withdrawal from Vietnam. On July 3rd of the same year, Radio Hanoi announced the release of three men in recognition of Independence Day in the United States. Despite Hanoi's promises, the U.S., and the families of all men then known as POWs, spent an agonizing thirty-two days waiting for these three unidentified men to be released. Finally on August 5, 1969, the men were returned to the U.S. and eventually reunited with their families.

On September 2, 1969, the first news conference was held with two of the three prisoners released by Hanoi for what turned out to be mostly propaganda purposes. Lt. Robert F. Frishman, USN, and Seaman Douglas B. Hegdahl, USN, both stationed at Bethesda Naval Hospital, were present to give personal statements and answer questions from members of the press. The third serviceman, Captain Wesley L. Rumble, USAF, was stationed at Travis Air Force Base Hospital and was not able to attend the conference.

After reading the entire transcript of the news conference, it was obvious that the responses to certain questions were somewhat evasive. It was also evident that Frishman and Hegdahl had been "coached" by our government regarding the boundaries in which their responses must adhere, but understandably so. Yet within the seventeen-page transcript, clear and concise evidence from first-hand accounting clearly defined the conditions our POWs were forced to endure. We still did nothing.

By not adhering to international agreements, Hanoi was convinced it could exert pressure on U.S. public opinion to withdraw U.S. Troops from Vietnam. Hanoi was playing a cynical game with human misery, and they won. Tough, ruthless rules of political games prevailed over the simplest feelings of solidarity and humanity. Refusal by the North Vietnamese to release the names of American POWs or permit an impartial inspection of the prisons, which detained our men, was far beyond barbaric. Even the notorious war criminals of Germany and Japan respected the provisions of the Geneva Convention. Hanoi had stated repeatedly, however, that they would not release any information on the POWs until the United States made a full withdrawal of troops from Vietnam.

Why did the U.S. wait so long to do anything about the conditions in which our men were being held? Why did their families suffer years without knowing if their son, brother, father, or husband was dead or alive? Why did we as a country not demand Hanoi act in accordance with the Geneva Convention for Prisoners of War? And, lastly, but possibly the most critical question of the entire war, why did Congress not allow a full declaration of war so that Vietnam could have been fought as a war and subsequently won, instead of as a hands-tied political power struggle on a very costly playing board? The answer to these and millions of other questions regarding Vietnam can be answered quite simply. There existed no political opportunity at the time these crises occurred and, therefore, no interest from the U.S. Government in pursuing the issues.

As a nation, we will never know how many American soldiers and POWs went to their deaths alone because no one found it politically opportune to help them. Most of us will never know the gut-wrenching heartache family members experienced during the long years of not knowing the fate of their loved ones. And what of the men held day after day, year after year, in the jungles and prisons of Hanoi? How do we explain to them that their lives were in jeopardy, their families tormented by the unknown, their futures forever altered, simply because there was no political opportunity to warrant intervention by their own government? I can only retrace my steps and ask this question: Who was playing the most ruthless and inhumane game? Hanoi, or the United States?

As an undeclared war, Vietnam instantly tagged our captured servicemen as "political criminals," and "criminals of war" against the Vietnamese people. In this situation, the communist prisoner policy sets forth that political criminals have no rights afforded them by Vietnamese law. This was the response given to countless U.S. and foreign delegations and speakers when they attempted to press the general provisions of the Geneva Convention to which Hanoi officials signed June 28, 1957. To the manipulative and sadistic minds of the North Vietnamese authorities, however, the result of an undeclared war by the United States was seen as an aggressive and unprecedented act. This act, therefore, became the ammunition Hanoi needed to ignore the general provisions and treat captured military personnel as they saw fit.

The stakes of this political game increased daily as more U.S. servicemen were listed as Missing in Action or captured. The question still goes unanswered as to why, with all the intelligence information available and with first-hand recounts from released prisoners, did the United States not react intelligently and strategically to intercede and end the inhumane treatment of our prisoners? It appears quite clearly that when the political pawns, the lives of our captured servicemen, were dependent upon our next move, we ignored the opportunity present to win the game. Instead of enacting a full declaration of war and throwing our opponent completely off the board, we simply turned our heads, forfeited our move, and allowed North Vietnam to play by their own rules. This, as in most issues confronting society, brings about yet still another question. When did the people of America agree that Congress and other politicians could play God with our lives and the lives of our men in service? Maybe the political powers in office during Vietnam should have spent a few years chained in a jungle cage or locked in a black cell in Hanoi.

In November of 1969, and after two and a half years of captivity in the jungle, the prisoners of Camp 102 were told they were going to be sent north. The United States was planning to invade Cambodia, and the Vietnamese knew about their plans. In preparation for the invasion, the POWs had to be moved to a more secure location. Half of the now twenty-four prisoners in Camp 102 would make the journey north, and the men were excited about leaving the harsh jungle conditions. The prisoners had no idea what lay in store for their future, but in their own thoughts, whatever it was, it had to be better than the living conditions they now tolerated.

On the morning of November 8, 1969, thirteen POWs were removed from their tiny huts, blindfolded, and had their hands tied behind their backs. This had become common practice to the men, and after thirty months in captivity, they were glad to be leaving by any means available. "We would walk from about 8:00 a.m. until 4:00 p.m." Nat recalled. "I wasn't in very good shape, but then none of us were." Dressed in their black pajamas and Ho Chi Minh sandals, the prisoners began the long march north. They were suffering from beriberi, diarrhea and dysentery, mal-nutrition, and many had open sores and wounds that refused to heal. Having been confined to stocks for so long and without the luxury of exercise, the men were weak, and their limbs lacked the ability to function properly. These combined physical limitations made the move that much more strenuous, and the days to follow would be something the men would never forget.

Chapter 8

48 Days of Hell

Anice long walk in the woods where nothing exists but you and nature in all its glory. The beauty of the trees as sunlight plays peacefully through the clusters of leaves and branches. The gentle crunch of twigs breaking under exploring feet while the sound of birds and other small creatures fill the air with soothing music makes for an adventurous walk. Up ahead, a small stream greets you to provide a cool, thirst-quenching drink for a parched throat. Most people would gladly welcome the opportunity to spend a few hours or days exploring the wondrous beauty of a forest, but when force and torture enter the equation, tranquility and serenity evaporate.

"I was glad to leave the jungle on my trip to North Vietnam," Nat recalled one quiet afternoon. "We didn't know we were going north until a couple of days before we were to go. They gave me the back straps to my sandals on the day we left." The Vietnamese kept the back straps to the prisoner's sandals to prevent the men from escaping. "We were also given our usual bowl of rice and soup. Then we were tied and blindfolded and began [what would eventually become] the forty-eight-day trip. I carried my mosquito net and blanket tied up and strapped on my back while on the trail, plus I had a rice ball about the size of a baseball for lunch."

"When we left the jungle on November 6, 1967, we were all ready to go mainly because it would be different. The weather was good that time of the year. There wasn't that much rain, and the terrain wasn't that bad when we left. The first few days was rough, though, because of the [bad] shape I was in, but it was better than being in the stocks. I wasn't in very good shape, but then none of us were. We walked from about 8 o'clock in the morning until around 4 o'clock in the afternoon. It wasn't that steep in the beginning, just mostly level with some rolling hills. There was a lot of undergrowth and jungle grass, and there were days we would walk through elephant grass for hours. We also went through a lot of bamboo and small bushes on each side of the trail. After about two weeks, we got into hilly terrain. The trail was well used, and it reminded me of the Appalachian Trail."

There were twelve men who left Camp 102 in the first group to venture on this long journey, and Nat was among those twelve. The second group that headed north consisted of four men. Don McFail, Gail Kearnes, and Billy Smith, and another man whose name Nat couldn't remember, left shortly after the original group. Billy Smith had been deathly ill while in confinement and actually had leeches coming out of his nose, as his body was so badly infested. With his sickness showing no signs of improvement, Billy had become a liability to his captors. "One morning they [the guards] got up and took Billy to the latrine. The others heard gunfire, and then they never saw him again. The guards had shot him dead. He was just so weak and all, they just got rid of him. I think they [the other prisoners] said they had been on the trail a week or ten days when that happened. No one ever saw him again, or his body."

To Nat, the country in Cambodia and Laos was beautiful, especially in Laos. For the first few days of the journey, the prisoners were marched through thick, triple canopy jungle. On occasion they passed through open fields and patches of elephant grass reaching heights of eight feet. In other areas, the undergrowth was so thick the men could barely continue with their journey forward. The Vietnamese, familiar with the terrain, could slip through the jungle easily, while the POWs, weak from disease and malnourishment, had a difficult time at best. Enemy guards pushed the prisoners hard and fast through the tangled undergrowth and across sharp stakes and snags broken from earlier foot traffic. Hemp vines, used for securing bamboo poles together for the hooches, hung from trees of the triple canopy and slithered along the jungle floor, while thick stands of bamboo and nipa palms choked the already near invisible trails.

The first section of the trail was relatively flat and made its way perilously through the thick canopy. However, the farther north the group traveled, the more they noticed the scenery beginning to change drastically. The terrain grew steep and torturous, while the jungle grew even more dense where it was encountered. "We had to pull some really steep mountains," Nat stated, while remembering the difficulties of the trip. "Time went fast at first because we were all excited about being outside, but it was not easy walking being tied and blindfolded. There were days we could barely go 'cause we all had sore feet, and most of us were weak, but it was still better than being in our jungle cages."

"One good thing about being on the trail," Nat said, "I got more food to eat, and it was better than what we had in the camps. I guess they knew we had to have more food to eat to keep our strength up. They were also trying to impress the high ranks of NVA if they saw us. I got a rice ball for lunch... It was just a ball of rice about the size of a baseball. They didn't give us much water on the trail. When we would cross a river or stream, I would fall in just to get water. A lot of the times, the guards would yell and hit us when we did that. I will never forget, though, we came into a camp one afternoon, and the camp commander was very friendly. He told us we could have all the food we could eat. Hell, I had been there over two years and had never had all I could eat. That night I had rice, bamboo shoots, and some kind of canned pork. I had had it on Christmas once before. We all ate 'til we were stuffed. The commander watched us and told us we would be sorry. Well... We were, and that's the truth! We all got sick from having eaten so much, and the guards had a busy night. We all had diarrhea... God, we went all night long."

"The next morning the commander told us, 'You are Americans. That is the way most of you act because you are greedy. I just thought how stupid and brainwashed the commander was. The meal was good as it went down. I actually have some good memories while on the trail. One time the guard we had got sick and also had diarrhea. All of us had a good laugh, but he didn't think it was so funny. It made me feel good, though, to see the guard get it because I had been laughed at for over two years for having diarrhea."

The jungles of Vietnam hid many secrets from the public eye, and the vast majority of those secrets remain forever lost within the tangled mass of vines, trees, and government cover-ups. *Our* government, not the government of Vietnam. While our servicemen were sitting in rancid cells and jungle cages literally starving to death, the United States was shipping rice and bulgur wheat to Vietnam. Provided by the U.S. Agency for International Development, burlap bags filled with nourishing grains were shipped by the tons to various locations throughout North and South Vietnam.

As the POWs marched north along the Ho Chi Minh Trail, their stomachs cried out for food that would sustain their bodies and allow them to survive just one more day. Instead of more food, though, our prisoners were forced off the trail in many places to allow columns of NVA troops heading south to pass with supplies and provisions. From under their blindfolds, the tired eyes of the POWs gazed upon bags of rice being carried *to* the enemy, *by* the enemy. To add insult to injury, written plainly on the side of the bags were the words: 'Donated by the people of the U.S.A.'

What could possibly have been going through the minds of our POWs as they were chained and shackled together, praying for rescue by U.S. Forces? Yet, instead of a rescue, the men witnessed U.S. dollars being spent to provide the fuel that would wound, kill, and imprison even more of our soldiers. One simply cannot imagine the feeling of betrayal these men felt upon seeing those bags of rice. Young American men, fathers, brothers, and sons were dying by the thousands in a political war that made no sense then and still doesn't to this very day, yet their own country was feeding the enemy that in turn was stripping these same men of life.

Where is the reasoning and justification for the United States to have provided this fuel to their enemy? An assumption could be made perhaps that it comes from the POWs, themselves. No, they didn't receive any nutritional values from the contents of those bags, but they did gain *something* from them. After the enemy had consumed the rice, the bags were occasionally given to our POWs to be used as mats on which to sleep on the jungle floor. In trying to reap a positive aspect of this situation, a sad but very realistic conclusion can be drawn. The printed burlap bags would be as close as the POWs would get to the U.S.A. for many years to come. "I never saw the bags," Nat recalled, "but some of the guys did and told us about them."

"We walked the famous Ho Chi Minh Trail from Cambodia to North Vietnam. While we were on the trail, we would pass NVA soldiers for days—just a continuous line of new soldiers going south as replacements. It was unbelievable. I guess we were in Laos for about a week when we passed them. They would make us get to the side of the road. There were hundreds of them, and sometimes we would pass by and some would kick and hit us. I was cussed I know, too. I was usually hit on my legs below the knees. I walked for days passing only NVA soldiers going south. They all had new weapons and everything."

"We walked all through Cambodia and Laos, then back to the DMZ into North Vietnam. For days we walked the trail, then the trail became a road. It was still the Ho Chi Minh Trail, but in places it was a road with trucks running on it. They would hide the trucks during the day and run supplies at night. We were put on the trucks late at night when we got to ride. We didn't know what to expect because the U.S. bombed the roads at night because they knew that was when they [the NVA] would run supplies."

As the men trudged ahead, streams of misty light striped the jungle air, as they pushed their way through the tangled undergrowth. Long, stringy vines hanging from the jungle canopy wrapped their hairy tentacles around tree limbs, forming a natural noose as the prisoners helplessly clawed their way forward. Shaggy, bare-leafed limbs slapped at the bodies of our men, stinging their exposed flesh like a hive of angry bees. "One of the worst things on the trail was being tied and blindfolded and trying to cross some of the rivers and bridges that they [the NVA] had. We crossed some bridges that was twenty-five to thirty feet high. Some were just a big log... It was hard to walk. All through Laos and Cambodia, a lot of the bridges we crossed was bamboo swinging bridges. They was rough as hell to cross! Some of the streams we crossed was rough, too."

During times of heavy rain, the ground became a red sucking mire of mud, making each step more laborious than the last. There were so many hazards along the trail during the day, but it was under the cloak of darkness that true fear was confronted. Numerous times the prisoners were forced to cross a river or stream, and their bodies became a succulent feast to the leeches just waiting for their next meal. After emerging from the water and disappearing back under the triple canopy, a velvety blackness pressed against the faces of the men and pushed their spirits to the very depths of despair. A heavy fog rolled off the river and spread through the jungle, gliding silently among the trees and chilling everything it touched. Fear rode heavily on the shoulders of every man, while deep in their guts the POWs fought against all odds to keep their sanity on this long, life-threatening journey.

Crudely cleared brush and undergrowth that had been haphazardly slashed down left sharp, stabbing snags as the men made their way perilously along the trail. The thin rubber sandals issued to the prisoners offered no protection to the tender feet of the captured Americans. Constantly the thorns, snags, and jagged edges of the tangled undergrowth ripped unmercifully at their flesh and left swollen and infected sores. At times, the men passed strangely shaped red flowers pressed into the mud or lying scattered on the dry red dust. Upon closer examination, the weary prisoners realized it wasn't flowers they were seeing. The small images were drops of fresh blood lost from the men's feet as they pressed on deeper and deeper into enemy territory.

During his years in the jungle, but especially on the long march north, Nat would call on his inner strength gained from roaming the mountains of western North Carolina. A born woodsman, Nat's skills at hunting and fishing gave him an advantage other prisoners did not have. From years of ginseng hunting, when poison ivy and white sumac had to be avoided, Nat soon learned to recognize and avoid most of the toxic plants in the jungle. Fellow prisoners, who were only familiar with asphalt jungles, had a more difficult time with the terrain and contacted with the poisonous sap excreting from crudely slashed undergrowth, causing them untold misery.

Debilitated from torture at the hands of the enemy, and nearing starvation from the lack of nourishing food, the spirit of these proud Americans fought an unending battle to remain alive and intact. The conditions the men were forced to face clawed at their last efforts to survive and remain sane while trudging along the trail. Tortured

68

flesh cringed from each forward step where the ground could not be clearly seen, knowing that biting black and red ants, poisonous snakes, and endless scores of leeches waited for the prisoners to fall victim to their waiting jaws.

Nighttime seemed to be the most lonely and frightening time for the prisoners. Deep within enemy territory and virtually lost to the rest of their peers, the few men who survived captivity had only each other from whom to draw strength and the determination to live from one day to the next. Passing through the Highlands along the trail, the lowly caravan walked through Montagnard territory. Known as "Yards," the men were rugged tribesmen, their women bare-breasted, together trying to dig out a living in the harsh elements and nearly barren soils of the Highlands. The teeth of the Montagnards, like those of most Vietnamese, were black from the chewing of betel nuts. These nuts provided a numbing effect on teeth that were devoid of any care, while the reddish spittle they produced followed the chewers like small trails of blood along the jungle's floor. At night, though, Nat recalled sitting in the temporary camps along the trail and listening to the eerie sounds of the Yards' music as it floated down the mountains and up from the valleys, tugging at the heart strings of the prisoners. "They played stringed instruments shaped something like a dulcimer," Nat stated. "The music was similar to the bluegrass and folk music we have around here in the mountains. A lot of times, we could hear the Yards down in a valley singing and playing. It was not good on my morale. It was some of the most lonesome music I've ever heard and sure did make for some long, lonely nights. It made me homesick."

"At night we pulled the blindfolds down, but I wasn't untied for the whole forty-eight days. We got more food, more rice and some soup, like that water lily or sewer greens soup. Sometimes we got rice or corn in it, but, when we had the soup, it was something like real thin grease, and we poured it over the rice. They usually had a hut they put us in every night so they could watch us, but by the time we ate we was wore out. They gave us a handmade spoon to eat with. It was just an old spoon made out of Babbitt, something like aluminum that you could mold and shape it easily. I wish to hell I had brought mine out."

"We would stay over a day in some of the camps [along the

trail], and during those times a lot of the people around the camp would come to look at us. We were like monkeys in a cage. A lot of the people, the Dinks, would try to get to us to beat us. I was hit several times. I know in one village a big mamasan came at me with a pitchfork. The NVA let them hit on us some, then there were others who would give us a cigarette and be friendly." It was difficult for Nat and the other POWs to contemplate their treatment from one moment to the next. At times, some of the Vietnamese along the trail seemed friendly and tried to show at least slight compassion for the shackled men. Others, however, tormented them by spitting on them, hitting the men with sticks or broken handles from farm tools, beating them with their fists, or hurling rocks into the group of helpless captives. The cruelest treatment came from those who had lost family members or friends from assaults by other U.S. Forces. While the feelings and resentments shown by the Vietnamese were understandable, Nat and his weary companions suffered unmercifully, and often unprotected, at the hands of their aggressors.

Just about every two days or so the group would end the day's walk at a camp set up along the Ho Chi Minh Trail. Among these were two different types of camps, the Liberation Camps and the Socialist Camps. The Liberation Camps belonged to the Viet Cong and were way stations made up of crude lean-tos with a place for the prisoners to do their own cooking, but not much more. This particular group of prisoners, however, never had the opportunity to cook, as they were constantly blindfolded and in handcuffs. The Socialist Camps, on the other hand, belonged to the North Vietnamese and were highly organized transit stations. These were the worst, as the prisoners were more closely guarded, and there were more soldiers at these particular camps.

Airstrikes by the U.S. brought a mix of hope and fear to the prisoners. "When an aircraft would be flying in the area, they would stop and hide us. Sometimes we would stay hidden in the undergrowth for two to three hours. I would walk for several days then and never hear a plane. Usually when an aircraft was in the area [it meant] the U.S. had spotted enemy movement, and usually there would be several air strikes. One time, I know it was in Laos, we were taken off the trail for four days and the NVA got upset.

70

The U.S. must have thought they [the NVA] had some prisoners with them because there was a lot of action from our side. The U.S. Forces was doing a lot of recon, so they may have spotted us. There was a lot of airstrikes that time."

"After we got into Laos, we had been walking for about thirty days, we then started to move at night. We were put on trucks and moved. That was probably the worst part of the trail. About every night we was on the move, and the U.S. was doing airstrikes. It made for a long night. While moving at night we rested during the day... We slept some when we could... But while moving this way, it was unreal how good the NVA hid their trucks during daylight. The Ho Chi Minh Trail turned into a two-lane highway in Laos before we went back into North Vietnam. The U.S. had done a lot of bombing on the road, but the damn NVA kept it open so the trucks could keep running every night. It was a scary time riding [those trucks] a lot of nights because of the bombing. I've seen the airplanes bombing in front and behind the truck that I was on. Damn, I had some very wild rides a lot of times. I was tied and blindfolded most the time though."

"I remember one night they were going to put us on trucks. There were two trucks together, and they put half of us on the first one. The driver of the second truck hated us and refused to let us ride. We watched the first truck go out of sight, then just about that time the [U.S.] jets came in. The second truck took a direct hit and exploded just as it drove off. Thank God I wasn't on it. With all that bombing I thought, 'Damn, they're gonna get us.' They came close, they really did. We was never in a bunker except that one night when they put us on trucks and the second one got blown up. They put two of us in each bunker. My God, it was growed up! They put Newell with me, and one would look at the other and wonder who was going down that damn thing first. It hadn't been used in a long time and was all grown up. I figured that it had snakes and stuff in it, but we didn't see any. We didn't sleep none, though. I guarantee you we didn't sleep none that night! We wanted to just lay on the ground beside the bunker, and told them if a strike come in we would jump down in it. I don't know where they was at, but they didn't get in it with us. But we didn't sleep none that night, especially after the snakes had crawled across our legs so much in the jungle. I could just imagine a damn Cobra or something crawling across you, 'cause you couldn't get out. That was the only time they put us in a bunker on the whole trail, but that was enough!" Nat laughed at remembering how scared they were. "Hell, I'd rather be hit as meet one of them. The U.S. dropped bombs the rest of the night, and it seemed like morning would never come. The next night, though, we caught a ride on another truck. Hell... I would have rather still been walking!"

"We caught up with the other guys in a couple of days," Nat continued. "They all thought we were on the truck that got hit. Even the guards were glad to see us. We had a cook we called 'Dinkleberry.' Hell, he went nuts, jumping around and jabbering in Vietnamese because he just knew we were dead. He was glad to see us, I guess. A lot of the guards probably would have been glad if we had been on that truck. That was one of the worst times on the trail, having to ride the trucks across the DMZ. The truck drivers drove like a bat out of hell, but they were liable to be hit by an airstrike at anytime. There were a lot of switchbacks on the road, and the trucks would have to back up. Damn, that was scary as hell. Another time, I remember when we were on the edge of North Vietnam, the truck I was on slid out of the road. We were all on the lower side of the truck. The guards all laughed, but they finally let us get out. The damn truck just about flipped over. If it had, the six of us would all probably have been killed."

"I know one time when we were at the DMZ, we were in the truck and our driver nearly scared us to death. They usually had four guards on each truck--two in front of the bed with us, two behind, and one in the front besides the driver. We were going up this steep mountain road one night. The driver, he would pull up, and you had to back up, anyway, and he killed his engine, and, hell, we rolled back until all we could see was sky down through there!" Nat was laughing hard remembering this. "He finally got it cranked and on around the bend we went, but, God, like I said, we had some scary rides, especially when we came back from Laos at the DMZ heading back north. They drove like something crazy, anyway, course I guess I would, too, 'cause you never knew when they [the U.S.] was gonna bomb," Nat laughed again. "And the damn guards, hell, you never heard such damn jabbering when he almost backed over that cliff," Nat stated, almost choking on his laughter. "Hell, I think they was ready to jump! They finally got it going, but they was a lot of prayers said that night!" Trying to catch his breath from the laughter, Nat continued. "That was just a regular night. It was a sharp switchback; it rolled back far enough that all you could see was space! Hell, we was tied and blindfolded, but we had them pulled up enough so we could see, and they, hell!"

"The worst part of the road was through the DMZ. There was no vegetation, no life, no nothing in the DMZ. It had been napalmed, and there was nothing but bomb craters." After marching for days through thick, lush jungle vegetation, this section of the trail resembled something from a horror story and yet depicted the very life to which the American prisoners were being subjected. The large stands of giant trees were gone, burned by the napalm dropped by U.S. Forces. Nipa palms and elephant grasses, that so heavily forested the ground previously, were now nonexistent and replaced by burned patches of soil and huge bomb craters. Through this area, the prisoners had no cover from the burning sun, nor from the airstrikes directed in that area by the United States. Each day as the sun began to set and air turned cooler, the prisoners would feel the layers of heat working up from the powdery red dust as they trudged slowly forward.

"After we got through the DMZ and into North Vietnam, it was safer because North Vietnam was not being bombed. The U.S. had halted the bombing in that area. It was a lot easier traveling, too. There was one time, I guess we had been there maybe the second day, and they put us in a station wagon." At this point Nat started laughing so hard he could barely tell the incident that follows. "It was me and Newell and McMurray. The station wagon looked like a damn hearse. You know how station wagons were, they didn't have no back window in it." Choking on laughter Nat tried to continue. "Anyway, they put us in it, and put me and Frank and Newell in the front seats and McMurray in the back." Still more laughter erupted at this point. "They put Mac in the back," Nat said, "and ol' Frank told him, 'We done got social 'cause the colored always rides in the back!'" By this time, Nat was almost beyond finishing the story from laughing at the teasing they gave their good friend. "That was the damnedest station wagon though; it was like those old 'Woodys' back in the 40's. The tailgate you let down just like a pickup truck, but it was like chains on both sides to let it down, but without a window in it. They was two or three trucks, and they was twelve of us, so they put so many on the trucks, and, hell, I was standing at the end of the line and got put in the station wagon. We rode it about half a day, with Mac bringing up the rear! I better not say what Mac's reaction was to Frank's comments."

"Once we got into the north, all the villagers would [come out and] watch us. I guess just to see what Americans looked like. We saw more farming, and a lot of rice paddies, and where they raised vegetables. I remember one day after we crossed into the north, an NVA soldier even gave me a pack of cigarettes, so we all smoked them. We rode trucks from there to our camp that was outside Hanoi. We got to the camp, which we called D-1, on Christmas Day, 1969. Once inside the camp, I was untied, and the blindfold was taken off. I had worn them ever since we left Cambodia, and I had just about got used to them. We had been on the trail forty-eight days."

Taken somewhere on a jungle trail by an unknown French photographer, this photograph would be the only hope Nat's family had that he was still alive. Two years after his capture the photograph was shown to his parents who identified Nat as the third man from the right. The identification changed his military status from Missing in Action to Prisoner of War, but Military Officials did not officially recognize Nat as alive until about two months before his release in 1973. From left to right: Martin Frank, Nat Henry, Frank Perricone, and Stanley Newell.

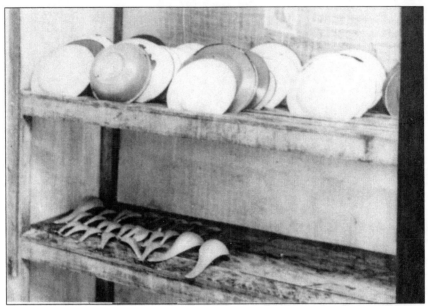

Above: Dishes and spoons used by the prisoners at Hanoi Hilton.
Below: Left behind at Little Vegas, a part of the Hanoi Hilton complex, two POWs flash the sign of victory as they know freedom is close at hand. These two men were part of the last group to leave the Hilton.

Above: Only moments from freedom, Nat is the first of his group to board the waiting C-141 at Hanoi's airport. Billy Beard is the next POW in line while NVA guards monitor the process.

Below: The faces of freedom. 34 men comprising the third group to leave Vietnam reveal stunned elation after boarding the US plane headed for Clark Air Force Base in the Philippines.

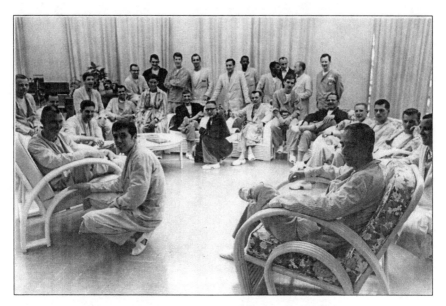

Above: Clark Air Force Base, Philippines. A few days later the members of this group would return to the United States and to the families they left behind. They were finally free men.

Below: A young well-wisher holds a sign waiting for Nat as he flew into Fort Gordon, Georgia where he would see his parents for the first time in 6 years.

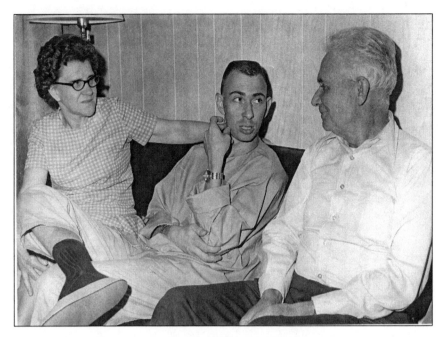

Above: Back with Mom, Arcilla, and Dad, Thurman at Fort Gordon,
GA after almost 6 years in captivity.
Below: My "pajamas" and Ho Chi Minh sandals.

Above: Nat and Danny O' Daniels going through some of the many gifts awaiting Nat's return.
Below: The "Freedom Tree" and presents provided by family, friends, and well-wishers.

Above: Finally back home with Mom and Dad in North Carolina.
Below: At home in North Carolina with the entire family and a family friend. Left to right: Nat's brother Harry, his wife Mary Ann, his older brother Pratt and his wife Cora Lee, Nat, a family friend Bill Parish, and Mom, Arcilla and Father, Thurmon.

Above: Nat's medals: Two Purple Hearts, Two Bronze Stars and One Silver Star.

Below: The original four POWs: Martin Frank, Nathan Henry, Cordine McMurray, and Stanley Newell at a reunion.

SSgt. Nathan B. Henry, U.S. Army, Ret.

Chapter 9

Camp D-1

D-1 was initially a holding camp for prisoners moving north, but with the progression of the war and an increase in the numbers of American prisoners taken, it soon became a regular prison camp like most of the other facilities in and around Hanoi. Upon placement within this camp, the newly arrived prisoners were issued new prison clothes. Nat recalled, "The camp commander, 'Snake,' and some guards came into the room with new PJ's." The pants and shirt were gray with black letters on the back of the shirt and down the side of the legs. "Each one of us had a different number. I never knew why they done it because it didn't make sense," Nat said. Not understanding their placement, the men tried to decipher the meaning of the numbers; but, try as they might, no rational explanation could be determined for their sequence and order. "Hell, we looked at those numbers over and over trying to figure out what they meant," said Nat. "We knew there had to be some kind of meaning to them because they all looked the same. It took us all of a year to finally figure out what they meant. It was our birthdays turned backwards." Nat took out a piece of paper and demonstrated his assigned number. "My birthday is 05-13-47, but it was on my clothes as, 74-31-50."

"After arriving at the new camp they separated us," Nat

84

continued. "I was put in a room with four other Americans. All our morale went down when we were put in the dark cells. The five of us stayed together, though, because we had been captured out of the same company. One other guy [in the group] had been captured a year later. That first night, Christmas night, we were taken to the camp commander and given a cigarette and a couple of cookies. He told us we could sing Christmas carols, but I damn sure didn't feel like singing carols. He told us how good we were being treated by the Dinks and all the bull about how they were winning the war. The day after Christmas, we were allowed to get a bath and shave, and, of course, we had to hear all about what good treatment we were receiving."

"This camp we named D-1. We also called it the 'Black Walls' because the walls of the rooms were painted black and had a solid door with a four inch by four inch peephole in it so the guards could check up on us. We had to bow to the guards in the jungle when we went outside, but here we had to bow every time the guard came to the door. In this camp, any time a guard would look in, we had to stand up and bow. Lots of the guards would look through the hole several times while on duty just to make us stand up and bow. I bowed a lot because they didn't like the way I did it. We were not allowed to lie down until 9 o'clock at night. It made a long night waiting until the bell would go off, and the guards would check every few minutes to make sure we were still sitting up so we could bow."

"The first week at D-1, we were interrogated just about everyday. It was the same old shit we had in the jungle. There were other POWs In the camp, but we never saw them close enough to talk to them. It was all about what units we was in and what kind of operations we was on. They told us that we had been captured since '67, and about all the lenient treatment we had received since then. They said we needed to make statements and tell the American people how wrong they was and all for starting this war. They would bring those danged old books in for us to read. We had to study the Vietnam history and all about when the French was there. We were told that they [the NVA] would beat the United States the same as they did the French because their people were so much more dedicated to their country where the American people were not. Then they would bring some propaganda [literature] back to our rooms for us to read. After we had read it, where most didn't, the camp commander would come and want to know how we liked it and would tell us why it was important that we had read it. Then he opened it up and would ask us, for example, what was in the first paragraph of page 129, etc. Well, I couldn't remember some stupid question like that. Then he would jump up and down and say that we lied and that we hadn't read it. A lot of times we would have to read it again. But I never did read the whole book, mostly I just glanced at it. This went on for quite awhile, but finally they gave up on us and just said we were brainwashed Americans."

"We had to stand up a lot, especially in D-1. Every time the guard came around, we had to stand up and bow. If you was laying down when they come in and didn't get up, then you had to stand up and bow, sometimes up to twenty times a night. We didn't stand up that long 'cause soon as they would shut the window, we would lay down, and then when we heard them coming again we would jump back up."

How was morale in this new camp? "Most of the time morale really got low in D-1," Nat commented. "I mean, my God, you couldn't see out, and we had already told all the tales we knew in the first two camps. Someone would start to tell another one, and someone else would say, 'No that ain't right, you told it different the last time.' Tempers got really short. There was never no fights, but we would get mad, then whoever got mad wouldn't say nothing for the day. I mean, tempers really got short. At least in [camps] 101 and 102 we could at least see sunshine and at least get out, but, my God, in that damn dungeon you couldn't see nothing! When we would go out, you know, to even get our meal, after you had been in that dark room for so long, the sun would really hurt your eyes." You had to go get your food? Nat nodded then replied, "They brought our food to the door, but would make us walk out and get it. They wouldn't bring it into the room. It was the same way in the jungle. They had a hut built, and they would bring the food to the hut, then someone in the hut would go out and get it. It was in a wooden bowl-like thing. We each had a little dish we eat out of, but we got to where we had one guy, it didn't matter who done it, but we would all sit down and measure it out. People were so hungry, and when you start

86

reaching in to get your share, you know, you would get a little more, so measuring it was the only way to be fair, 'cause tempers got short over that, too. People would say, 'Damn, you got more than I did,' and after everybody would round their bowls up [with rice], then that last one, he wouldn't get but a third of a bowl. We usually took turn about filling the bowls level, then took the spoon and knocked it off, then, by God, it was level! But that way everybody got the same. When you get hungry like that you get greedy."

"After I got to D-1, we were given bread instead of rice... It was a nice change. The food in the north was a lot better than in Cambodia, but still wasn't nothing to write home about. The soup wasn't no better. We had punkin' soup an awful lot, too." Boiled, unseasoned soup of pumpkin, cabbage, or "sewer greens," as the POWs called them, was a typical meal for the captured Americans. Often infested with vermin, the soups were fed to the prisoners for months at a time with no other food to accompany the insipid liquid. The men received two bowls every day when these items were in season. Just imagine, for three months, twice a day, you received nothing but rancid soup. That would amount to 180 consecutive bowls of pure dread with no flavor, minimal nourishment, and a contributing factor to diarrhea, dysentery, scurvy, beriberi, and hepatitis. Due to the filth and unsanitary conditions by which the POW's food was prepared, the men contracted whipworms and tapeworms that plagued them constantly. Whipworms needed to exit the body to lay their eggs, and often the men would wake up at night to the feeling of worms crawling out of their rectum. This became an unavoidable condition, but often the POWs would try to laugh it off or compare sizes of the worms just to make the situation more tolerable.

Remembering the bitter cold of winter at D-1, Nat revealed this next thought. "It was around February of 1970, I guess. It was so cold in this camp that we even slept together trying to stay warm with all of us on a three foot wide bed of wood planks. Newell and I slept together for a good while until it got warmer. I will never forget the first night that we slept together. The guard looked in the peephole and went to yelling because he couldn't see all of us. He didn't know that Newel and I was on the same bed board. They called out, and the officer opened the door, and they all come in looking around, then went back out the door mumbling."

The floors and walls of Camp D-1 were solid, thick concrete, and the dampness that hung in the air penetrated through the walls and floors making the cells even colder. The prisoners were not given extra blankets at night or extra clothes to guard against the bone-chilling wind and damp air. They had no socks to wear on their feet, or gloves for their stinging hands. Once again, the only comfort they found from the cold was in huddling together as best they could and trying to survive the winter weather.

Which would you say was the worst, the black cells at D-1 or the cages in the jungle? "The black cells," Nat stated emphatically. And why is that? "Hell, you couldn't see out. I mean it was dark really all the time. They had light bulbs, but they never cut them on. Time really went slow in this camp. The only time we were outside was to get a bath, and that was once a week. I was confined to that dark room all day. We got up at 6:00 in the morning and went to bed at 9:00 at night. We had to lay down in the middle of the day. They had a bell that would ring to get up by and to go to bed by. I had to lay down when the bell rang at night. I also had to lay down of a day whether I would sleep or not."

"I had been in D-1 about two months when we were taken to see a movie. It was about when the French was in Vietnam....the same old propaganda. I often wished I was back in the jungle while at D-1, even if the food was better here. I stayed here for about eleven months. I think it was in May or June of 1970 that the camp commander came in our room and told us we could make ourselves a mattress. They gave us a sheet that had been sewed up. I made mine and used it about three or four days. It was hot then and trying to sleep on it was impossible. I think the guards knew that, though.

"Another thing we got here was that we got to hear the radio. We had the camp radio at D-1, and we got to listen to it maybe once a week. It was all Hanoi Hannah, telling how many planes they shot down and how many they had captured, and how the United States was losing the war, and all the usual bull. Every time we turned around, too, we had a shake down. They checked everything we had about once a week or sometimes every two weeks. Snake and the camp guards would come in the room, and we would have to stand while they searched our beds. They would go through them, our PJ's, and everything else. I remember one time I had made a toothpick from a piece of bamboo. I had got it smoothed down and sharp on one end. The guard found it and gave it to Snake. He called me to the interrogation room and raised hell. He said I had a very bad attitude and how sorry we all was because we had tried to kill the guard in the jungle. He acted like I would try to kill and hurt a guard with it. He said when the war was over I would be held and tried as a war criminal, but I had heard that a thousand times already. They told me a lot how bad my attitude was, too," Nat recalled.

How did you learn about the communication process like tapping, etc.? "We didn't know about it until we got to D-1 and learned it by talking through the walls. They watched us so close there, too, that it was impossible to do the tap code. It was real hard to communicate with the other prisoners. We tapped on the walls anyway, but evidently no one could hear us. When we went to the latrine, we couldn't pass notes because we were watched very close. The walls were very thick, and that made it hard to communicate. We tried to talk, though. I used my water cup pressed against the walls to talk, 'cause my voice has always carried good. D-1 was the hardest camp I was in to communicate."

"I got sick one night and I layed down before the gong went off," stated Nat, "so the guard we called 'Shitface' opened the peephole and went to yelling for me to get up. I sat up and he left, then I layed down again. He came back and yelled again. The next morning I was taken to see Snake. He put me in solitary confinement for three or four days, then took me back to my old room. I had been at D-1 for eleven months I guess. This was the longest eleven months I ever saw."

"I guess the longest I ever stayed in solitary at one time was from ten to fourteen days, but I was in solitary several different times. If you screwed up, they put you right in there. Some of those guys stayed in for three or four years... I don't see how they took it, I swear I don't. Tempers got short with the ones you were with after a while, but when they *did* put you in solitary, time went twice as slow, especially if you were handcuffed and in leg irons, too. Every time I ended up in solitary they handcuffed my arms behind my back and then put my legs in leg irons. Hell, you couldn't lay down. All you could do was sit."

"I guess it goes back to my dern stomach. I had a really bad stomachache, and it was hurting way up under my rib cage. It didn't get no worse being put in solitary, but it sure didn't get no better. The rooms in D-1, when they put you in solitary, they couldn't have been over six feet by eight feet. They was so small. It seemed like the walls was blacker in them small rooms, and then you was in there by yourself, and that made a big difference. When they put you in there, you couldn't lay down at all. Normally you had to lay down during a certain part of the day, but in that one you couldn't. You had to sit up. You had to set on your bed and lean against the wall. They made you stay up during siesta time with the rest of them, too. I guess that was just more punishment."

"On Christmas of 1970, we got another good meal, and some of the guys sang Christmas carols, but a lot of us didn't. We were always told how good the people was to us, and we should show respect to the people of North Vietnam for all the good things they were doing for us. Then the third Christmas came and went, and it was no better than the first two."

Chapter 10

It Should Have Been Us

Twenty-three miles west of Hanoi lies Son Tay Citadel. A mosaic of rice paddies, irrigation ditches, and a canal that flowed just north or the compound's west wall, comprised the countryside surrounding the camp. The Song Con River flowed so close to the walls it often threatened to flood the camp, yet its very presence made the prison cold and extremely damp. The winters at Son Tay were the hardest, fueled by the cold of the river, the cruel lack of medical care, barbaric torture, and starvation. Inside the walls of this compound were seventy American POWs suffering from severe deprivation at the hands of their captors.

With buildings named the Opium Den, the Beer House, and the Cat House, Son Tay was inhabited by early shoot-downs captured between 1965 and 1967. The camp was activated on May 24, 1968, when the first group of twenty prisoners was moved from Hoa Lo in Hanoi to Son Tay. Shortly thereafter, forty-five more men were moved in from Hoa Lo and other nearby prison camps, bringing the number to sixty-five. Over the next two years, five more men would be added to the roster. Being a "working camp," Son Tay was a sad and dreary place for the POWs held within its confines. But in an exemplary demonstration of their unconquerable spirits, the sun broke through heavy clouds on Thanksgiving Day of 1968, and the

91

prisoners decided to nickname their new home Camp Hope.

In May of 1970, President Nixon was facing some of the most difficult days of his presidency. A full-scale invasion of Cambodia, approved by Nixon, divided the American people when it failed to yield little more than the discovery of sixty-five tons of rice. Only days earlier, four students had been killed, with eleven more wounded, by National Guardsmen at Kent State University. The Secret Service had surrounded the White House with bumper-to-bumper buses in an attempt to keep out seventy-five thousand protestors demonstrating against the war in Vietnam. It seemed as though the nation was falling apart, and yet just about the only thing Americans weren't divided on was the POW and MIA issue. Everyone wanted them home, but the North Vietnamese were not going to release their hostages until the United States withdrew all forces from Vietnam. Although Nixon had begun to pull out the troops, there were still over 428,000 servicemen throughout Southeast Asia. Something had to be done.

That same month, yet unbeknownst to the president, plans were getting underway for an operation code named "Kingpin." This operation would consist of a surprise helicopter raid on the Son Tay POW camp in North Vietnam and would be conducted by an elite, handpicked U.S. Special Forces rescue team. Donald D. Blackburn, an Army brigadier general, was the SACSA (Special Assistant for Counterinsurgency and Special Activities) to the Chairman, Joint Chiefs of Staff, who headed the operation. From May of 1965 to May 1966, Blackburn had headed one of the most secret, elite units in Southeast Asia known as SOG. The public was told SOG was a Studies and Observations Group, when in reality it was a Special Operations Group consisting of handpicked CIA operatives and volunteers from Navy SEAL Teams, Air Force Special Warfare Units, and Army Special Forces. Blackburn, later stationed in the Pentagon, wanted a "hunting license" to enter North Vietnam with his Special Forces Troops in order to take out the Lang Chi hydroelectric dam sixty-five miles northwest of Hanoi. After reviewing evidence sifted from tons of intelligence data, Blackburn felt Son Tay might just be the license he was looking for to prove the ability of his SOG units. Alongside Blackburn was Army Colonel "Ed" Mayer who headed a small group within the SACSA organization called the Special Operations Division. Blackburn, together with Mayer and a small, carefully chosen group of top-secret advisors, planned the raid on Son Tay, taking extreme measures to insure its secrecy and accuracy, and to focus on every intimate detail of the operation.

To execute this operation, a select group of the Army's best-trained Special Forces personnel would be assisted by Air Force pilots flying helicopters nicknamed Jolly Green Giants. Wearing maroon-colored berets, the men who were to accompany the Army's Special Forces units on this mission were some of the sharpest para-rescue men in the Air Force. As plans detailed, while the Army and Air Force executed the planned assault, a Navy air diversion near Haiphong would provide the necessary confusion to North Vietnamese radar and tracking devices to allow successful air penetration by the raiders. With the best "weather window" for the raid falling between November 20 through 25, the long-awaited plans were about to be executed.

After months of precise top-secret planning, the time to make a final "go" decision was approaching. Despite intense efforts to obtain the most accurate and reliable information for this operation, problems began to surface. Conflicting reports filtering into Washington's data collection centers kept the planned mission on hold. Reconnaissance photos from SR-71s over Vietnam were taken from altitudes of 80,000 feet and above, yet the photos were so sharp that a skilled interpreter could count the exact number of people within the walls of a compound. Just before the planned raid, an SR-71 that flew over the Son Tay prison camp found the only cloud within a mile centered directly over the target area, preventing a clear shot for analysis. Reconnaissance drones, also known as Buffalo Hunters, flew at treetop level gathering critical images of the target the SR-71s could not obtain. Of the seven Buffalo Hunter flights over Son Tay before the launch date of the raid, six of the flights either malfunctioned or were shot down. The seventh flight banked too soon and returned with a beautiful shot of the horizon just *beyond* the Son Tay camp. The latest photos used to determine activity within Son Tay would be eight days old, of marginal clarity, and producing a fifty-fifty chance that anyone was in the camp.

Were prisoners still being held in Son Tay? That was the critical question to those few participants organizing the operation. DIA (Defense Intelligence Agency) experts, CIA officials, and numerous other government entities produced cables, photos, and messages that on one hand stated, "the prisoners were there," while on the other hand, the same reports said, "they're not there." Officials in charge needed and wanted the planned raid to be a success for many reasons, and the final decision to "go as planned" would be the most difficult decision of their careers. Failure of this operation could lead to a public outcry against military practices and against an already frustrated presidency. If news of an attempted rescue leaked out, officials feared repercussions from the NVA against the Americans already in prison camps. Not to mention demonstrations on the White House lawn just six months earlier were still fresh on everyone's mind. A successful raid, however, would boost public morale nationwide and provide a crippling blow to the North Vietnamese, possibly forcing them to resume the Peace Talks in Paris. Either way, the decision to raid Son Tay prison was about to be made, and it was too late to turn back now.

Wednesday, November 18, 1970, President Nixon was briefed for the first time concerning plans for the Son Tay raid. After mulling over the idea, later that evening Nixon gave his approval for the raid to take place. On Friday, November 21, 1970, at 2:18 a.m. Hanoi time, the first HH-53 helicopter appeared over the walls of Son Tay prison. With exact and carefully planned timing, a C-130 flare-ship dropped its flares, and the entire area exploded in brilliant light, illuminating the area for the raiders.

"I will always remember November 21, 1970," Nat stated. "It was just a normal day for us, same old routine. I remember it was a clear day. We all heard the sound of a helicopter, then we heard some small arms fire. I didn't know what was going on, but the sound of choppers sure sounded good. It was scary at first, though, when you heard all that damn gunfire coming in. Hell, we thought we was getting rescued and cheered them on when we heard the small arms fire. That really pissed the Dinks off! We all clapped and cheered, and, oh God, they would get mad. All the guards went running around, and they would look in the peephole and holler at us. We didn't realize that the U.S. was making a raid on a POW camp, or that they were raiding a camp that had no POWs in it."

Flying into the center of the Son Tay prison courtyard, the rescue teams were confused and disheartened to find the camp completely

94

empty. It was now painfully evident that six months of grueling strategy sessions and preparations had just produced negative results. Despite precise, intense training and perfectly orchestrated plans, fifty-six men had been sent deep into North Vietnam only to come up empty-handed. Unbeknownst to all of the Special Forces personnel involved, the prisoners being held in Son Tay had been moved to another prison almost four months earlier. Planners in Washington had suspected for a long time that the camp was empty, but their desire to execute this plan was so intense that the men physically involved in the raid were not informed of the suspicions until after the operation was complete. Regardless of the outcome, though, the courage and dedication of the Special Forces men was exemplary of planned secret operations, and credit needs to be given as such.

"They [the NVA] came with our evening meal," Nat recalled, "but said nothing to us. D-1 was fairly close to Son Tay because we heard all the noise, but it stopped almost as fast as it started. If only they had hit our camp, maybe we would have been rescued. When it got dark that night we heard trucks. Snake and the guards came in and told us to get our shit together. We were moving."

Elation in hearing the choppers was bittersweet for the prisoners when coupled with the thoughts of 'It could have been us.' "They tied and blindfolded us," Nat continued, "then put us on trucks and moved us closer to Hanoi. We were taken to Plantation Gardens. On the ride to the Plantation, I tried to look under my blindfold, but couldn't see much, except that we were somewhere in Hanoi. Probably on the outskirts. We could hear traffic and passed a lot of people. After we got to Plantation Gardens, I guess about three or four weeks later, and they got the communications going, we found out what really happened [at Son Tay]. The information came from Ted Guy, the SRO (Senior Ranking Officer), 'cause he said he knew where the Son Tay prison was, and one of the other guys already there was in it, and that's how they figured it out. After we found out, we wished they had hit our camp."

Chapter 11

Where Cotton Was King

The Plantation. The epitome of southern style, grace, and bar-b-ques on the lawn. Sprawling mansions with manicured lawns and soft rolling fields filled to the brim with bolls of cotton ripe and ready for picking. A place where time moved as slowly as a lazy river and blossoming magnolia trees enhanced the quiet serenity of hoop skirts and ascots. A loving home for the elite aristocrats; a showplace for passersby; a living hell for others. From the pages of history, an era long since passed, the Plantation came to symbolize the Old South where 'Cotton was King ' and a person's worth was determined by their wealth and by the color of their skin.

In Vietnam, The Plantation brought about a completely different meaning. As one of the most well known sections of the Hanoi Hilton, Plantation Gardens was, in itself, a hell on earth. The Plantation had been the home of Hanoi's Vietnamese mayor during the French occupation. In the center of the walled compound was a two-story yellowed stucco colonial-style villa, similar to any of the nicer homes in Vietnam. This villa served as the camp staff's offices and quarters, and had rooms with tiled floors and fireplaces. The POWs called this the "Big House." It contained the interrogation room and had a large bomb shelter outside.

Overall, The Plantation looked like a large warehouse that had been divided into small cells housing from one to ten prisoners. The cells ranged in size from ten feet by ten feet, for solitary confinement, to twelve feet by twenty feet, for multiple prisoners. Each cell was lit by a dim, naked light bulb that burned twenty-four hours a day. Completely bare except for wooden planks that served as a bed, the floors were tile or concrete, and most of the ceilings were covered with square yellow tiles. Several barred windows with French-style louvered shutters that were locked tight divided the walls. Each cell also contained a 'Liar's Box'. This was a vibrating radio speaker, located just out of reach over the door, which broadcast the Voice of Vietnam, the official radio station of Hanoi. Here also reverberated the voice of Hanoi Hannah with her stinging renditions covering the progress of the Vietnamese against U.S. Forces. Although her words rang out with vile propaganda, it was very effective against the men forced to listen to her seductive, yet venomous, voice.

On the east side of the compound was a long building the POWs code-named "the Warehouse." Judging from the hooks hanging from the wall, the POWs figured that was exactly what it had been during the mayor's time. To the south were outbuildings, probably used for former servant's quarters named "the Gunshed." Toward the north were even more outbuildings converted into cells and called "the Corncrib." An area called "the Movie House," that was later used to show outdoor propaganda movies to the prisoners, was on the west side of the compound. A small and very worn courtyard of pressed gravel was located near the Warehouse and contained a basketball goal at either end. "At The Plantation, there were different names for each section," Nat recalled. "We had the Corncrib and Gunshed, and some called the building I was in The Warehouse."

With the current Senior Ranking Officer [SRO] beaten and imprisoned in a section of the camp where it was impossible to communicate with him for guidance, the camp needed immediate action from the next SRO. Some of the prisoners had been released and sent home based on an existing camp policy that the wounded and sick could go home first if offered release by the North Vietnamese. In turn, those men who had been captured and held the longest would follow by date of rank. Col. Ted Guy, the next SRO in line, felt no one should go home regardless of the situation or date of rank. He felt the prisoners were all in this mess together and would all go home together, either dead or as the proud Americans they were. Morale was shattered within the camp and Col. Guy had a long and arduous task before him.

On March 22, 1968, U.S. Air Force Lt. Col. Ted W. Guy was attacking an automatic weapons position over-looking Route 9 (Ho Chi Minh Trail) in Southern Laos, when his Phantom F4C sustained heavy damage and went down. Guy engaged in a firefight with fifteen North Vietnamese regulars, was wounded, and subsequently dragged and hauled approximately three hours to an enemy camp. After several hours of beatings and treatment beyond belief, Guy passed out. The next morning he awoke with not only a strong desire to survive, but he also realized at that point that he would need to establish a personal code to abide by if he were to accomplish this goal. For the next several years, Col. Guy would follow the Military Code of Conduct plus these two personal codes he made to himself:

- I would resist until I was unable to resist any longer before I would do anything that would embarrass my family or my country.
- I would accept death before I would lose my honor.

Guy was determined to survive against all odds and would later instill this same passion in the men he would command throughout his years of captivity.

In July of 1968, Col. Ted W. Guy took over as SRO for The Plantation and immediately took action to restore order within the prison camp. During this time, there were forty-three Navy and Air Force pilots and one Navy enlisted man being held within its confines. Through notes and tapping methods, Col. Guy issued seven directives to be followed by all POWs within that camp. They were simple and followed along the lines of the U.S. Military Code of Conduct:

- To back all U.S. policies
- Resist as much as possible
- Accept no personal favors or gratuities from the enemy

- Remember your American heritage, that you are an American and proud to be one
- Do not write
- Do not tape (record)
- Do not go home early

Time would reveal that Col. Guy paid an exorbitant personal price for his efforts to maintain these directives and discipline within the ranks of prisoners he commanded. Guy spent forty-two and a half months in solitary confinement while a prisoner of the North Vietnamese. After serving months in solitary at Plantation Gardens, Col. Guy was again beaten and tortured for ten days, then placed back in solitary for another four months. He was told that the reason for this treatment was that fellow prisoners had stated to their captors that he was encouraging them to resist.

Whether the information was given freely or extracted through torture, Guy's efforts were obviously paying off, and it infuriated the North Vietnamese. By early 1969, order had been restored by Col. Guy, and a higher morale was returning to the POWs. The second week of December of the same year, Ted Guy was consolidated into the Hanoi Hilton along with the other forty-four prisoners. Guy had suffered a dislocated shoulder after his capture, was debilitated from dysentery, and his body weight had fallen to ninety-five pounds. Despite his physical condition and endless days of solitary confinement, Col. Guy continued to communicate with his fellow prisoners. The North Vietnamese caught him communicating again, and on June 10, 1970, Guy was transferred to yet another and more isolated prison eighteen miles southwest of Hanoi. Once again in solitary, Col. Guy was now at Camp Farnsworth, or, as the other prisoners called it, Camp D-1.

In the evening hours of Thanksgiving Day, 1970, Guy, Nat, and the other prisoners now being held in D-1 were driven back to Plantation Gardens. The Plantation had been vacant for more than three months, and from this time until close to the end of the war The Plantation would be used mainly as a prison for Americans captured in Laos and South Vietnam. Many of these captives were enlisted soldiers, and, for the most part, no one in the U.S. knew whether these men were dead or alive.

To prevent any communication, Col. Ted Guy was placed in the Gunshed on the south end of the compound. The majority of the time he was the only prisoner in that section and was kept in total isolation. There was a tremendous psychological advantage to being in communication and having someone else to lean on, talk with, and carry on discussions no matter how trivial the topic of conversation. When someone was in solitary, a special effort was made by the other prisoners in camp to communicate with that man and always to let him know that the rest of the camp was with him. Strength and unity was a universal belief among the POWs. In many cases, the Vietnamese thought if they removed the senior man, then communication chains and structure among the prisoners would fall apart. They couldn't have been more wrong. Any time the senior man was removed or isolated from all communications, the next highest man would immediately take over and communication would resume its normal activities.

When you were moved from D-1 back to Plantation Gardens, what kind of COM efforts did you use to communicate with Guy, since he was in solitary confinement when you arrived? "We hadn't been there over a week when we got COM from Guy about passing the notes in the latrine and bath and tapping on the wall. That's the first place we learned about the tapping... We knew about it in D-1, but the walls were so thick you couldn't use it effectively. My voice always has carried good, so I was the one that did all the talking. I would place my cup up against the wall and I'd try to talk at D-1, but it was a hard place to communicate in."

"When we got there, [to The Plantation], Col. Guy set a Como line, and it helped a lot. Col. Guy had also been [with me] in D-1. The morning after we got there Snake and Cheese [the guards] came in and told us we were moved because the U.S. was up to their old tricks trying to beat the NVA, and how they out-smarted the U.S. Their [the NVA] intelligence was very good. Better than the U.S. would probably admit. We were all interrogated by the Cheese. They always tried to get us to make tapes downing the war, but I always refused."

The Rogues, or more commonly known as The Peace Committee, were a group of men who showed a "good attitude" to their captors. These men wrote letters and made tapes for the North Vietnamese stating their objection and opposition to the war, and met the demands of the interrogators in order to receive "special" treatment while imprisoned.

"It was here that we first heard of the Peace Committee," Nat recalled. "There were eight or ten men who thought the sun rose and set on the Vietnamese. It would make me sick after all I had been through from the jungle camps to the march north, then to see and hear these guys. Hell, they were allowed to stay outside all day and got more food, cigarettes, everything. The Snake and Cheese would tell us to get a good attitude and repent, and we could be like them and get treated as they did. That damn bunch wrote all kinds of propaganda and made all these statements and tapes [against the war]. The guards was always with them talking and telling jokes. The whole camp just overlooked the whole damn group. Hell, no one had any use for them."

"The early part of '72, I think it was, Jane Fonda came to our camp. We knew someone was coming 'cause we had to hang out a blanket and a pair of pajamas to make it look like there was more in camp than there was. She came to the Big House, but we never saw her. They took the peace group over and they did see and talk to her. They were like two peas in a pod. She walked through the camp, and we was hoping like hell she would come toward us, but she never did. We just wanted to see what she looked like."

The vast majority of the POWs was not in agreement with the members of the Peace Committee and deeply resented those few men and their blatant collaboration with the enemy. The others would see the Rogues outside most of the day enjoying the fresh air, receiving extra food, cigarettes, and even beer supplied by the North Vietnamese as a reward for their cooperation in making propaganda statements and tapes. Resentment toward the Peace Committee by the other prisoners often spurred retaliatory actions by the POWs that resulted in severe torture and punishment. Nat related one particular incident that happened to him which brought about a week of horrendous, debilitating torture.

"I had had a couple of seizures, and they [the NVA] moved me to a room they called 'the Sick Room,'" Nat said. "There were four other POWs with me: Gail Kerns, Billy Beard, Tom Kobashigawa, and Danny Hefner. Gail had been wounded in the head and was crippled up pretty bad. Tom had been burned real bad from a helicopter crash, and Beard had nerve damage and could not control his bowels. Hefner had back problems from a helicopter crash, also."

"We were in a room next to the peace group, and we were allowed outside like the rest of the POWs, but the Peace peace group was out all the time. Hell, them damn things would be out all day, and, hell, we might get thirty minutes. We had been in this room maybe six or seven months. So one day they let us out for about an hour, then we all agreed we wouldn't go back in when the guard came." Nat started chuckling at himself and at what happened next. "Then the damn guard came, the one we called 'Shitface,' and I said, 'Hell, we ain't a going in.' I was sick, but I wasn't as bad as the other guys, and I thought we was all gonna stand there. Of course me and my big mouth, you know, I spoke my peace and said I wasn't going back in!" Nat started laughing harder. "I refused along with Hefner, and told him [the guard] 'no' twice. Well, he went to running off in unknown tongues, then called either Snake or Cheese. They come and told me, 'You will be put in solitary if you refuse again.' I did refuse again, then I looked over my shoulder, and everybody was going back in but me! They [the other four POWs] were all in the room but Hefner, and he was standing in the door. They put Hefner in solitary in the next room over, and then he had an appendicitis attack that night, and they had to operate on him. So, they put him in the room next to where we was at and had to leave the door open. Everybody was going back and forth to the latrine, and they seen him a laying in there in a hospital bed and figured they [the NVA] had beat the hell outta Danny. But, hell, they didn't see me for a week! They didn't know what had happened to me."

So what happened to you for refusing to go back to the room? Nat laughed and shook his head remembering those next few days. "They moved me out of the camp and put me in leg irons and handcuffs. They took me out so quick I didn't know what was going on! We was headed in the direction of the latrine and bath, and, hell, I didn't know what they was doing. When we got outside the gates, we went to the left into a real small alley, and when I got there they blindfolded me, then they took me on out. You know, all the camps are kinda right there together, so I don't know where they took me, but it was a room maybe five feet by five feet and had no light. You couldn't see nothing. There wasn't no bed or nothing to lay on, so they just set me in the floor. The cell was a little bitty thing, concrete floor, no windows, not even a peephole. The guard put me in leg irons, then he handcuffed my hands behind my back. He said, 'You be sorry,' and left. You had your legs straight out with the leg irons on and, hell, you couldn't go nowhere!" Nat laughed slightly. "You sure couldn't get up or nothing, and if you fell over you was just stuck there. Damn, it was dark in there."

"In about an hour, Snake came in and told me I had a very bad attitude now. He said, 'Why you do this?' I told him if the peace group could be out, we should be, too. He hit me and said, 'You must repent,' and left. It was about noon when this all started. That evening I was given a small bowl of rice and nothing more. No water, either."

"I stayed in this place for three days. The third day, the guard came and got me and moved me back to the Gunshed, or whatever that was called where Colonel Guy was at, but I was still in solitary. They moved me back late that night and kept me handcuffed and in leg irons that night. I didn't have a bed there, either. They took that out when they brought me back, hoping I would go ahead and make the tape. You know, you had to set up against the wall, 'cause you was afraid to lay down. Then the next morning the one called Cheese come in and said my attitude was bad and all and that I was an American aggressor and all that stuff. He said, 'You will make a tape and apologize to the Vietnamese people.' I said, 'I ain't a makin' no tape,' and that's when they brought the stool in."

"They tied me to the stool, then tied me and put handcuffs and leg irons back on me. They put you on this damned old stool about that big, [Nat indicated a circle about ten inches in diameter], and you was afraid to move, 'cause, hell, if you moved one way or the other and fell off, they, hell.... I sat there all that day in my cell, and when they came and fed me and untied me, they took the handcuffs off just long enough for me to eat, and damn they was tight!"

"I stayed on that stool that one day. There wasn't no bed or nothing, so after that I just sat on that concrete floor. I finally got up against the wall and that was the way I sat. If you were to roll over on your side you couldn't get back up! I was tied up and handcuffed for two days, then they called me to interrogation to make a tape again. I said, 'I ain't gonna make no tape,' so they took me back finally and took the leg irons off. I went one day then with the leg irons off, then the next day they took the handcuffs off. Then they called me back again to interrogation and they still wanted the tape. I said, 'I ain't gonna make it, but that I would apologize to you as Old Cheese, but I ain't a makin' no damned old tape!' They took me back to the room again and took everything off, so I stayed that way for another day."

"After four or five days in the Gunshed, I was sent back to my old room with the other guys. They, hell, everyone thought I had died! I was gone a week altogether, I guess, six or seven days. Guy and them down there [in the Gunshed] knew that I had been brought back, but while I was gone, nobody else knew where I was or what had happened. This happened in the summer of '71, and although my resistance didn't help the situation, I made my point. I never did make no tape!"

What did the NVA do trying to coerce you into making those tapes? "They would call you over and give you a cigarette or two and tell you how good you had been treated and build up the Vietnamese. Then they would tell you how bad the American military was doing. Really what they tried to do was bribe you to get you to make them."

Were you able to communicate with Guy any while in the Gunshed? "Very little," Nat said, "'cause I was still in leg irons and handcuffs. We would have to walk out the door to get our food. Guy would come out and get his food, then I would haul off and go get mine. The Gunshed was like an L-shape, where I was on the end and Guy was in the corner where the L turned. Well, Guy would come out and he would cough or something. He knew I was over there, but as far as communicating, we couldn't. Not there, we were watched too close. I knew it was him, but all we could do was let each other know we were there. When we would go out and get the food I would say 'The damn things! It's over refusal to go into the room' and so on, just one word or a few words that would let him know what was going on."

"The routine went back to the same old bull. It was in The Plantation, though, where we really got the Como line to working good. It was a great morale booster. We would pass notes back and forth in our buckets. We always put notes in the lid of the bucket, and when we would go empty it, we would hide the notes in the edge of the latrine. We would always have to hide it fast because we was watched very close. Another way was by hiding the notes in the bath area. I found a piece of plastic in the courtyard one day and slipped it into the room. We used it to wrap our notes in, and then place them in the plug of the water tanks. Both ways, one group would hide them and the next room would pick it up, and it would go through the whole camp that way. Especially the notes from Colonel Guy. Guy was a very good SRO. He always tried to help the morale of the others, and he always tried to keep up with all the POWs and what was happening to them. I have a lot of respect for the man. He was a military officer and a damn good one!"

"I remember, we would go take a bath in the bathhouse. I would always go to the left, and they had a big room to the right, so we decided we would go to the right and talk to the [prisoners in the] Corncrib. So I went in that side that day, and the damn guards was looking 'cause they knew which side you was supposed to be on. Well, that first day went all right, then that second day me and Perricone went, and we tapped on the wall, and I got to talking. They could hear me in the Corncrib, but the guards did, too, so I didn't get to take a bath on that side no more," Nat laughed. "They didn't do nothing to me, though. It's a wonder they didn't, but nothing happened."

"I can't remember if it was Frank or not, but we had a note one day and were gonna hide it," Nat stated while starting to laugh. "The wash basin had a plug on the inside and the outside, so we pulled one out and put the note in. I don't know if there was so much force from the water or what, but it knocked the other plug out! They, hell, the guards went to jumping up and down while we were trying to get the plug back in it," he said, choking through the laughter. "It was a big old cement tank with water in it that emptied in a hurry when that plug fell out, so we had to stop passing notes that way. That was the best way to pass them, though, at least for a week or so, 'cause it had two plugs, and we could take one from the inside out and put the note in plastic and stick it back in." Nat laughed again, "There was water everywhere, though, and you couldn't get a bucket full of water to save you! You know, we kept that plastic the whole time we was there."

"In the fall of '71, I guess it was three or four months after the tape treatment, I had another seizure and what we figured was a

105

stroke. Whatever I had, it made my left side very weak. The stroke paralyzed my left leg and arm and my face. The feeling came back in my face and hand within twenty-four hours, but still my arm and leg wasn't working right. This went on for about three months when Colonel Guy sent me a message."

A message had been passed through the Com line to a civilian POW named Ernie Brace, stating that Nat badly needed medical attention. Ernie Brace had become Colonel Guy's chief communicator and had acquired the code name "Moses." As his name suggested, Brace passed on critical information from the SRO to the other POWs within the camp. In the note from Nat, guidance was requested as to whether he should agree to write statements for the North Vietnamese if that was the only way to get medical attention.

"Guy sent orders down for me to do whatever I needed to do to get medical treatment. He had seen me going to take a bath and swinging one leg out of control and flopping around. He figured I was in bad shape. I sent word back that I wasn't doing nothing! He was good, you know, he went through hell setting up the communication. He was tough. There were guys that was as bad or worse off than I was. All of us just had to tough it out. I never had to do anything to get the treatment, but they really didn't do anything but give me a couple shots. I guess it was vitamin shots or B12 shots, who knows? They thought it was some kind of miracle drug. Really, it just got better on its own. I always had the bad attitude, so I didn't get no special treatment."

In returning Guy's response to Nat's medical treatment, Ernie Brace was able to contact one of the men in the peace group. The information was relayed to Nat, but the member also informed the guards that Colonel Guy had personally issued the directive. This clearly proved to the North Vietnamese that there was an active command structure operating within the camp. The next day, Colonel Guy was taken to the Big House, where he was tortured continuously for the next ten days and nights. He was locked in leg irons, beaten with fists, flogged with a rubber hose, and kept in a kneeling position for close to eighteen hours. Sergeant Henry, on the other hand, was placed back in solitary confinement in the Closet. The men paid dearly for the leak in their COM line, but somehow the link to keep in touch with everyone must continue.

106

Chapter 12

Changes in the Wind

"In this camp we did get better treatment for a while. It probably was because of the Son Tay raid. The rooms were bigger at The Plantation," Nat recalled, "and we had tile floors here. They were damn big rooms. I guess they was fifteen by twenty-five feet. The rooms in The Plantation was cleaner, too, than D-1. We took an old pair of PJ's and wiped the tile floor every day, and we didn't wear our sandals in the room. They still had those damned old boards to sleep on, too. I remember one time, I guess it was about three or four months before we left, they gave us sawhorses, and we put our beds on that. You know, it was hard getting used to sleeping on that after being on the ground for so long. That's what they looked like though, just regular old sawhorses. They said that was showing their humane treatment."

"We had a much better bath area. We got to go out and get more exercise and take more baths here. We could get a better bath because here we had bathhouses, really. I had not had a good bath in a long time. It was a big concrete box and water was running into it continuously. We had about a three gallon bucket to dip water with. The water came out of a spigot and ran all the time. It was about four by four by three feet. You could stand up, and it would hit you about waist high, and you didn't have to bend over. You could take a damn good shower that way. They was rooms, I think about four small rooms then one big one. In each of the small rooms, about two men could take a bath at the same time, then in the big one about four could get in it, I guess. It was a whole lot bigger, but I never did get in it," Nat laughed remembering. "The big room was out on the other side of it, next to the cells, and they didn't let me get into it cause my damn voice carried so much. I could take that old tin cup, you know, that one we used for drinking and all, and I would turn that over, and I would talk, and my voice would just carry right on through the walls! They wouldn't let me take one over there, 'course that was because I got caught too many times talking through the wall!" he said through a chuckle. "I went in there one time, and Perricone went with me. I forget who the other one was, but, by God, they made us go back out and get in the other one 'cause they know'd good and well what we was gonna do. So I always got over next to the side that looked out over the railroad track. I couldn't talk there!" Nat exclaimed while still laughing. "We had gone so dirty in D-1, though, and this was a little better, but still...life at The Plantation was no bed of roses."

"They put ten of us in the same room here," Nat stated. "The guys in my room were the five of us that were captured together, plus Pete Drabic, Thomas Horio, Leonard Daughtery, and Jose Jacques. I can't remember the other guy's name, but we had ten [men] in this room, also."

"Time passed faster in this camp because we could communicate better here, and the atmosphere was better, but it was still the same old bull from the Dinks. We had been here about a month," Nat recalled, "when some 'big wheel' came to the camp. He was dressed up in his NVA uniform and shoes and the whole damn nine yards. He wanted to know how we were being treated and if we were getting enough to eat. He said we could get better treatment and food if we would show a good attitude. Hell, I had been told how bad an attitude I had since 1967, so the big talk didn't help them because we all just kept our bad attitude. One of the things the Dinks would say is, 'Why do you support your president? If he was a good man, you wouldn't be here.' The more they harped on it, the more I told them we had the best country and the best place to live in the whole wide world. I told Cheese if he ever got to the States, he would never leave 'cause he would like it so much. He got mad and said again that I had a bad attitude. I was also reminded that I would be held after the war and be tried as a war criminal, which I had also heard since my capture."

Nat sat quietly for a moment or two, then we chatted more about his stay at Plantation Gardens. "I remember they give us a checkerboard, but didn't give us no checkers, so we made them outta white paper. Instead of black and red, we had black and white, and for the black we took a piece of charcoal and made marks on one for the black, and the other one would be white. Then, after we got to The Plantation, we got a regular deck of cards. They would bring them to us and let us play with them some during the day, then take them back that afternoon."

"Ol' Frank, he kept every cigarette butt he could find. He would even pick up the butts outside. Hell, he had a sack full of tobacco! They give us that propaganda paper, and he would start rolling cigarettes, then when they give us a light that night for our cigarettes, then we would still be smoking two hours later. He kept lighting one off the other and kept one burning the whole time. Ol' Frank, though, he would pick up everyone's butts," Nat laughed. "Hell, he always had tobacco after we got to The Plantation. We found some more pieces of that plastic, and he kept it in that. Then we had them old propaganda sheets, and he would use that to roll them in. They usually gave you a cigarette, and you had to smoke it before you eat. When they brought the food, then they would give you a light. I don't know why they done it that way, but they did."

The prisoners were being treated slightly better by the end of 1972. Torture had all but ceased to exist; the men were receiving slightly larger portions of food; and their time outside the grim prison cells was increasing slowly. The men in captivity had only heard rumors over the past four years about the Paris Peace Talks, but something was about to change, and their treatment by the enemy proved to be the early signs of things to come.

On May 13, 1968, the Paris Peace Talks began formulating between North Vietnam, South Vietnam, and the United States in an effort to end the war raging throughout Southeast Asia. After opening formally on January 25, 1969, the talks to settle the war bounced back and forth between Le Duc Tho, negotiator for North

Vietnam, and Henry Kissinger, negotiator for the United States. The third party of the negotiations was South Vietnam's President Nguyen Van Thieu. Like a seesaw, the talks were up then down, on then off, with all three sides winning and losing major issues.

By October 8, 1972, the North Vietnamese appeared eager to get a quick settlement and made a proposal that met many of the requirements set forth by the U.S. With major talks taking place between Kissinger and Tho, a date for signing the agreement was set for October 31. However, due to premature words by Kissinger that "peace is at hand," plus a misunderstanding between both parties regarding the issues, the agreement remained unsigned and negotiations were on hold once again.

Frustrated by the lack of progress with the talks, Nixon decided to take matters into his own hands. In a letter to South Vietnam's President Thieu, Nixon's reassurance to "take swift and severe retaliatory action" should Hanoi refuse to continue with the negotiations set the precedence for the future of the talks. This statement represented a solid commitment by the United States to enforce the agreement by military means and hopefully bring an end to a seemingly endless war. Then on December 15, Nixon sent a message to Hanoi demanding they reopen negotiations within the next seventy-two hours or face immediate repercussions. Initiated for purely psychological reasons, the Christmas bombing of 1972 was designed to force Hanoi back to the negotiating table demanding an agreement be reached to end the Vietnam War. The bombing was designed to be a maximum effort to take out all military installations in and around Hanoi and Haiphong. Other facilities targeted were railroad yards, roads, steel works, bridges, and electric power plants. Originally planned as a three-day operation, Nixon extended the time frame indefinitely, or until the North Vietnamese demonstrated serious attempts to negotiate for peace.

Making good on his threats, Nixon began bombing on December 18, and continued through the twenty-ninth day of the month. Except for a thirty-six-hour truce for Christmas, the bombs continued to drop twenty-four hours a day. During this time, the Air Force and Navy mounted 724 B-52 sorties with approximately 640 fighter-bomber sorties, dropping a collective total of thirty-five thousand tons of bombs. Supporting aircraft included an additional

1,384 sorties that provided refueling flights, fighter cover, SAM suppression, and other efforts to assist the attacking aircraft.

"The United States started bombing just about everyday in the fall of '72. In November, we had to dig up the floor in our room and dig a trench. We dug it under our beds so the beds was over the hole. They bombed very close to our camp, and a lot of the times they were so close that the plaster would fall off the walls and ceiling. Just before Christmas, the B-52's really started doing their thing," Nat recalled. "They did some [bombing] around the first of December and more throughout the month, but the week of Christmas, the B-52's bombed around the clock. When they came in, you would just barely hear them, and then the bombs would start dropping, and it would shake the ground. It was all this bombing that [eventually] brought the North to their knees. The U.S. bombed all night Christmas Eve and about all day Christmas Day. There were times that the bombs got awful close to the camp. There was a railroad track behind the camp, and it was one of the targets."

Did you ever hear the air-raid sirens during the bombing of '72? "God, yes. It was about continuous. See, during Nixon, they bombed about around the clock. We'd heard 'em a few times back earlier. They had a few raids that come in back in early '72 or late '71. The first time we heard it, we didn't know what in the world it was 'cause they hadn't bombed up there. They had some air strikes from '68 on- - off and on, though. They mined Haiphong Harbor, but lot a times you'd hear that siren go off, then you'd hear a hum, and it would be a B-52 and, hell, it'd be in there before you knew it! You could barely hear the 'hum,' then the next thing you know'd the whole place was a shaking! There was a lot of fighter jets, too, but after the eighteenth when they started bombing in December, most of that was B-52's. If they missed it the first time, sometimes it would take three times [runs], but they got it," Nat laughed, talking about the targets of the B-52's.

Did you ever think it would hit your camp? "Yeah, a lot of times I really wondered. At Plantation Gardens, they made us dig fox holes in our cells, but then when we got to Little Vegas. I reckon by then they knew where every camp was at, but they got close. Too close for comfort a lot of times. You talk about lighting a place up when they went to dropping...my God! We could see all the flashes. It looked like a bad thunder storm," Nat laughed, "Sounded like it, too! You've heard thunder here when it rolls and rolls, and, my Lord, the earth would shake! I mean they would drop one— say this was our camp, [indicating the house we were in], and they would drop one as close as that field right over there," Nat stated, pointing to a large open field less than a quarter of a mile away. "That's too damn close for comfort! They got real close. But their [the U.S.] intelligence was so good, they had to know where every camp was at. They only damn thing about it was is that *we* didn't know *they* knew where we was! There was that big damn '*if*.'" Nat laughed, thinking of the uncertain feeling the POWs had during the bombing runs.

"On that Christmas Day, though, we got a better meal," Nat stated. "They gave us our 'Holiday Special.' We got canned pork and rice, and we got bread and all. We never got bamboo shoots after we got to the north, though. Course we had rice, too. It wasn't like the old rice we got in the jungle, though. It wasn't fried rice, and it wasn't boiled, but whatever it was it was good. On the holidays we usually got some kind of eggs, too. It was like scrambled eggs. You wouldn't get but just a little spoon full, then we'd all have diarrhea the next day or even that night," Nat laughed.

"The Vietnamese always celebrated Tet. To them, it was a lot like Christmas is to us. Each year, which was the beginning of a New Year, was given names like 'the year of the monkey or dog.' They always had a rice ball that was wrapped in leaves. I don't remember what all was in it, but it wasn't good. It was good to them, though, and was like ham or turkey to us on our holidays."

Nat recalled an incident that happened during the Christmas bombing, which he still laughs about to this day. "It was during this time I had a bad toothache. It was late one night, and my tooth was giving me a fit. It was abscessed and was one of my back ones. Hell, it had swelled up bad. They [the U.S.] was bombing that night, and Frank was rolling cigarettes. I got one of them, then when the damn guard came around checking, I got him to give me a light, and I told him I had the toothache. The next morning Cheese came in and asked if my tooth was still hurting. I told him it was, so about noon that day the medic finally came and told me they would fix my tooth. They came and took me down to this room. Well, they didn't have nothing but this big old toothpick like thing to look at it with, so they set me down and told me to open my mouth. There were two guards, and they grabbed my arms, and one grabbed my legs as I was setting there. Cheese was in there, too, and he said, 'You got toothache? We fix toothache.' He said, 'The dentist will take care of it,' and that's when they grabbed me! Hell, they fixed it all right; the damn dentist pulled it! After they pulled it, Cheese said, 'I don't think the tooth hurt no more,' and I said, 'I know damn well I'll never complain of the toothache again!'" Nat was laughing hard remembering this particular incident. "My face, neck, and whole jaw turned blue for about a week," he continued, while indicating the affected area along his jaw-line and neck. "They never gave me nothing for it, but they did put a piece of cotton in it. I'll tell you what, that damn doctor got a hold of it, and it come out, course I was pulling the other way, too!"

The prisoners in Plantation Gardens had mixed emotions about the bombing that was pounding the area all around their cells. Something important was behind the twenty-four hour assault on Hanoi, yet the men were still unsure of what it all meant. With their treatment growing steadily better each day, the prisoners knew something good had to be coming in the near future. Although emotions and hope for release were running high, the lack of confirmation that freedom was near made every second of every day seem to pass like hours. Despite the effectiveness of the bombing, though, a life without chains, bars, and dark depressing rooms would have to wait a little longer.

Chapter 13

The Hilton - Hanoi Style

"I think it was the last of December, late one day, when Cheese and the guards came to our room and told us that we were moving. They moved just a few of us at a time, and I remember it was just getting dark. We were tied and blindfolded as usual when they moved us. I was tied with Tom Horio, who had very bad eyesight. Well, when they started to put us up on the truck, he missed the step, and then down we both went! They all got mad over that, you know, they thought we just done it to aggravate 'em, but the poor old boy just couldn't see. We didn't get hurt, but it sure did make the guards mad. We were the last two to leave. They had done took everybody except us on our end of the camp. They was four or five on the other end of the camp they put on with us. They didn't take but five or six at a time, though, 'cause they was a guard for every one of us. That way we couldn't talk, plus they had us sitting here and there, and we just couldn't talk to each other. We were the last to be moved from The Plantation," Nat concluded, "and I was taken to the Hilton"

Pronounced "Wallow," Hoa Lo, or "Hanoi Hilton," as named by the American POWs, it was the infamous prison camp in North Vietnam where the majority of our POWs were housed. As the center of the prison network, Hoa Lo had served as a French Colonial prison for

114

Vietnamese criminals, many of which were high-ranking officials having served ten to twelve years themselves, imprisoned by the French and Japanese. Aptly named the "Devil's Island of Southeast Asia," Hoa Lo in Vietnamese meant, "the place of the cooking fires."

Broken wine bottles implanted in concrete ran along the top of the walls, where it interlaced with strands of an electrified fence that encompassed the Hanoi Hilton. The exterior walls of the compound were constructed using huge, white-washed concrete blocks ranging from one to two feet think, and, in places, towering to over twenty feet in height. The overall layout and structural content of the prison prohibited escape, especially with fourteen million people in and around Hanoi. A massive archway signified the main entrance where giant, wooden double-doors hung, bracketed with large iron bolts. The arch was laced with steel bars, while in multiple sets of three, barred windows covered with French louvered shades blocked out any light that dared to penetrate the prison's interior.

In kind words, the Hilton was putrid smelling. Years of urine, feces, vomit, and blood had seeped into every crack and crevice of the prison structure. It was inhabited by rats the size of small dogs, who often chewed the flesh of helpless prisoners at night or during debilitating bouts of sickness. Often the sickly prisoners had to fight the rats for their meager ration of food, but never more so as when it was placed outside their cell door before the guards returned to give the men their meal. Many times the POWs would watch helplessly through the cracks under their cell doors, while the rats, stray chickens, or other vermin devoured the precious few bites of food that lay just outside their reach. Huge flying cockroaches, mice, spiders, and ants invaded every square inch of the facility and contributed greatly to the living hell of the Hilton. There was no escape from the misery that plagued our men night and day.

During the long lonesome winters, the cold and damp of the concrete cells crept deep into the bones of the POWs, forcing uncontrollable spells of shivering. Yet, in sharp contrast, summertime turned the same cells into virtual ovens with temperatures reaching 120 degrees, wrenching sweat and precious moisture from the already debilitated bodies of our men. "The Hilton," as Nat recalled, "was a big place that had lots of camps on the inside of it. I will never forget when we went in. We went through the big gates and down a corridor that had a brick or cobblestone walkway. Once inside, it was a very gloomy place."

An eerie feeling of death wrapped its long, cold tentacles around the bodies of the POWs as they entered the massive doors of Hoa Lo, stepping from the bright light of freedom and into the deep, dark bowels of hell itself. As the huge wooden doors slammed shut, closing off the outside world, their sound reverberated fear and helplessness to the very souls of our American soldiers now held prisoner. Cold shivers fled through the bodies of our POWs, as they took their first steps into the mouth of hell and trudged down the corridor of its throat. Many, already incapacitated by their treatment during capture, were facing the most dismal journey of their lives. For Sergeant Nathan Henry, the sound of those same doors closing was nearly unbearable. An escape from the huge walls and tightly barred doors was now impossible, and all hope was shattered as the huge, bracing bar slammed loudly into the iron supports. There would be no freedom from this place.

Crude, inhumane torture that hurt beyond comprehension, beyond the limit of human endurance, became a daily threat to the POWs. Initial interrogations normally consisted of a session of savage beatings, where most of the newly captured Americans gave only their name, rank, serial number, and date of birth as required by the Geneva Convention. Debilitated by their captors, the prisoners soon realized the North Vietnamese were not only impatient, but also very effective in their extraction methods to obtain the information they wanted. Going "on the ropes" was the most common *and* most effective means of obtaining specific details the enemy wanted. With their arms bound behind them until their wrists and then elbows touched, a rope was then looped through the bindings, pulled up behind their necks, and then strung over a hook or bolt in the ceiling. Once secured, the rope was then pulled tight until their bodies were lifted off the ground. Many times, the shoulders of the prisoners were literally pulled out of their sockets with this method, yet the men were left to hang in this position until they talked. Some were able to hold out for a week to ten days, but eventually everyone was broken and gave more than the Big Four. An irony that plays into this torture method is that, in 1967, the ropes used by the North Vietnamese were actually replaced with nylon straps from the parachutes of downed U.S. Airmen. The new straps were stronger and wouldn't snap with the weight of the Americans, and thus our men were being tortured with parts from their own equipment.

On January 6, 1965, Navy Commander Robert H. Shumaker attempted to pass the first POW message inside the camp, but his attempt failed. Trying to send encouraging support to a newly captured POW, Shumaker scratched a message to him that read, "Welcome to the Hanoi Hilton," thus giving Hoa Lo the infamous nickname, the "Hilton." In the earlier days of captivity, communication was difficult at best. The men most commonly used the charred ends of a match stick and scratched messages on a piece of toilet paper, then left these messages under loose bricks at the wash basin or in a sewer pipe at the latrine for access by other prisoners. In order to establish communications with other sections of the Hilton, the men would scratch messages on the insides of the flat metal handles of their meal buckets, which circulated minimally between "New Guy Village" and the Hilton. Although limited success resulted from these efforts, it was a beginning, and gave comfort to the new arrivals that other Americans were nearby.

After spending 133 days in solitary confinement, Robert Shumaker received his first roommates. Seeing the need for an effective communications system, Shumaker, along with Air Force First Lieutenant Bob Peel, Air Force Captain "Smitty" Harris, and Navy Lieutenant Phillip N. Butler devised a system before they could be separated again. Harris remembered a tap code supposedly used by Korean POWs, and therefore the Vietnam POWs soon adopted the same code. Within a short period of time, the tap code became second nature to the vast majority of the American prisoners using this code to communicate between cells. Almost immediately, the code was expanded to fit the necessities of the men as a result of separations, guards, or other restrictions that didn't allow the use of 'tapping' as a means of communicating. The American POWs developed hand gestures, coughing, clearing their throats, or spitting that utilized the communications code. Other ingenious methods included sweeping a broom to the rhythm of the tap code, using a cup pressed to the wall, or even a hand-towel rolled up in the shape of a cone worked effectively. After the establishment of this communication chain, and when the POWs were separated, they taught other prisoners the code, who, in turn, taught still others. Listed here is a copy of the tap code used by the American POWs. The letter "K" was omitted from the alphabet to provide a succinct union of letters:

A	B	C	D	E
• •	• ••	• •••	• ••••	• •••••
F	G	H	I	J
•• •	•• ••	•• •••	•• ••••	•• •••••
L	M	N	O	P
••• •	••• ••	••• •••	••• ••••	••• •••••
Q	R	S	T	U
•••• •	•••• ••	•••• •••	•••• ••••	•••• •••••
V	W	X	Y	Z
••••• •	••••• ••	••••• •••	••••• ••••	••••• •••••

In addition to the tap code and related methods of communicating between cells, hand signals were also used. When the sound of tapping prohibited the necessary contact between prisoners, a "silent" method needed to exist to insure the continuation of the COM line. Hand signals became the alternative method used by the POWs. An illustration of those signals is listed below:

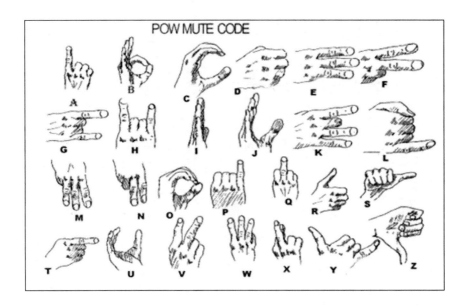

POW MUTE CODE

Within a relatively short period of time, the POWs had established an extremely effective system of communicating throughout the Hanoi prison system. Too much information was being exchanged between the prisoners, and it interfered greatly with the attempts of the Vietnamese to keep the men separated. As a result, the camp authorities began "COM purges" to determine how the Americans communicated. Severe torture and punishment was leveled on those men caught communicating, yet when someone reached their limits and had to relinquish COM information under enemy interrogation efforts, the prisoners just changed their com links. It became something of a game played between the prisoners and the Vietnamese.

Something that was *not* a game, however, was the fact that the prisoners were treated like animals during captivity. There was not a day that passed that the POWs didn't long for the comforts of home or the arms of their loved ones. Not a day passed when they didn't wish for a hot bath, a nourishing meal, or a soft bed upon which to lie. Their desires and longings were coming closer to a reality, and after the continued U.S. bombing in December of 1972, conditions within the Hilton began to improve slowly.

Once Sergeant Henry was placed behind the huge walls of the Hilton, changes started taking place in many areas. "I was taken to a place that was called ' Little Vegas,' Nat stated. "The rooms in this place was a lot bigger than in Plantation Gardens. I was in a room with twenty men or more. There was not much room outside, but we were allowed outside about like it was in The Plantation. In this camp, the rooms was much bigger and a lot more [men] was put together. They were fifteen by fourty feet, I guess, maybe fourty-five feet. They was maybe twelve to eighteen inches between the beds with about a four foot walkway. They still had them damned old boards, though, to sleep on."

"Time went slow in this camp when I first got there. The men that I had been with all the time was put in another room, and I was put with another group. We all knew each other, though, from being at The Plantation. We just talked about where we were from and the units we was in and stuff like that, but we didn't swap lies and tales like we did when there was just five or six of us. Then it was good later on 'cause time went a lot faster 'cause they was more to talk to and more to talk about. But, hell, nighttime was what was bad! You get twenty men in a room and them snoring! I'd walk the floor of a night and wake 'em up!" Nat laughed heartily. "I mean, God Almighty, some of them could really snore!"

"Things had gotten better at The Plantation, especially after Thanksgiving of '72, I guess it was," Nat continued. "We started getting more food, and it was a little better. We got a few more cigarettes, too, then after we got to Little Vegas it got even better. We would get a bowl of rice, and everybody wasn't fighting over the last grain 'cause there was more than enough. We got more meat, too. It was that canned pork, but damn it was good, though. It was just like regular canned pork, big chunks of it. We got that milk, too, that sweetened condensed milk. They just give us a little bit, but Lord it tasted good! We figured that since they signed the agreement, they wanted to fatten everybody up."

"It started getting better, though, about the time we got to Little Vegas. But we didn't get the pork until after the Peace Agreement. We got a lot of fried rice, though, instead of that regular stuff, and we got it about three times a week after the agreement, too. We got a lot more rice. We got bread most of the time in the north, and the pieces got bigger. It looked like a smashed out biscuit or something. It didn't really have that good of a taste. It was good, but it didn't have no flavor. I don't know exactly what it was made out of, but I think maybe it was wheat."

"I remember it was in early January that I got a bad case of the sore throat, and Stephen Leopold got hepatitis. The Dinks moved us to a camp close to Little Vegas, but they moved us plumb out of the camp! They was afraid the others would catch what we had. They had never moved me before because I was sick. I was lucky, too, that I didn't catch what Leopold had. Hell, the only thing I had was a sore throat or something, but Leopold turned as yellow as a damn punkin'! He actually had hepatitis. We didn't have to eat or drink the same water or food, they brought mine separate."

"I will never forget, though, they put us together in a little bitty room, and the street was just outside our cell. There was a small hole in the wall at the bottom of the cell. I guess it was like where they had left a cement block out, and we would lay there of a night and watch the street. They [the North Vietnamese] would ride up and down the streets and play that old music. Late at night, then we would watch the rats come out. You know, they didn't have no sewage system over there, it just run in the gutters and ditches of the streets. There was a lot of human waste, even in downtown Hanoi. I guess that's why there was so many rats. I saw them walking the streets at night as big as small dogs. Hell, that street would be full of 'em way up into the night. Dang, we hoped and prayed one would never come through that hole," Nat laughed. "We slept with one eye open, though, 'cause if you was to wake up at night with one of them things on you, you would have a heart attack for sure! They looked just like dogs running around... something like a wharf rat around here. God, they was weird looking! We were in this camp for about a week before we were taken back to Little Vegas."

"When we got back to Little Vegas, things began to get even more relaxed, and we were allowed outside just about all day. We was allowed to talk to the other prisoners, and the food got a lot better and [there was] more of it. All that I was ever with was enlisted men, though. I was in the room with the warrant officers, but never with the pilots, except Colonel Guy. They [the NVA] kept you separated. They would let us together outside, and I guess Little Vegas was the first time I ever got to talk to Guy out in the open. You know, we would slip and talk through the walls, but there they just

121

let the whole group out together. They knew the war was coming to an end and it didn't matter."

The "carpet bombing" of Hanoi worked as Nixon had planned and forced the North Vietnamese back to the bargaining table of the Peace Talks. Besides bringing the North back, along with a renewed hope to end the war, Nixon's bombing action brought favorable results to the American POWs. After intense negotiations during the first month of the New Year, the agreement was formally ratified on January 23, and then went into full effect on January 27, 1973, bringing to an end the longest war in history involving U.S. Troops. It would take, however, a little more than two years to get all combat troops and advisory personnel out of Vietnam.

Chapter 14

Wings of Freedom

"I will never forget the night of January 28, 1973, when we found out the Peace Agreement was signed," Nat recalled. "We had heard for years about the Peace Talks that was going on, so I really didn't know what to think. The camp radio came on and I expected the same old bull that I had heard for the past almost six years, but I realized that the war was coming to an end, thank God! Oh, God, that was good news, though. Hell, we stayed up all night! That was when I was in the 'Big Room.' That night everyone got all excited, and I doubt if many slept much that night. We talked all night about whether we was gonna get out. I bet there wasn't three people that slept thirty minutes that night, though. The guards, they really didn't say much about it until we tried to communicate with another camp next to us after the agreement was signed. The guards... They, my God, they hit the roof then, but there wasn't no way to communicate to the others except to talk. They knew it, too, but we was just trying to talk to them. Oh God, they got mad! They was all pilots in that other camp. I don't mean to knock them, but most of them got a whole lot better treatment than we did. Some pilots got it pretty bad, but others, it seemed, didn't get nothing at all. But none of us had a bed of roses... pilots *or* enlisted men. Some of them got to write home and receive packages, though. Mother said she sent packages once a month, and I guess the damn Dinks ate it or something, 'cause we never got nothing. No packages, no letters, not the first thing."

"After the Peace Agreement was signed the bombing stopped. We were all called to a room and asked if we would write something about how good our treatment was and how good we had been treated. They wanted us to tell the American people what the U.S. had done to the Vietnamese people. They wanted me to write, but I refused, so I still had a bad attitude, but that was nothing new," Nat grinned. "We were allowed outside all day, though, after the Peace Agreement was signed. The Dinks was all more relaxed. Even Cheese was more friendly, but that was probably because he thought some of the POWs would make some type of statement."

Did you ever write or make a tape? "I had to write one to the camp commander. I had to write and apologize for refusing to go into the room that one time. They wanted us to write something denouncing the war and all, but I never would. I wrote and told him I was sorry, but I thought it wasn't right. Peace Committee or not, we should be out, too. I had the bad attitude." Nat grinned. "As far as writing statements, though, I never wrote no statements, and I wouldn't make a damn tape for nothing."

After the agreement had been signed, select groups of prisoners were treated to visits to museums and theaters and given beer and wine to drink. These luxuries were offered during the last few days of captivity for the prisoners, as camp authorities tried to exploit the euphoria American captives would feel at the time of release. Lavish displays of "good" food accompanied by parties and photo sessions for some of the POWs, was an attempt to make the prisoners forget about their suffering and inhumane treatment received at the hands of their captors. But the Americans would have little, if anything, to do with this lavish display of pompous theatrics by the North Vietnamese. Their attempt to further show "lenient and humane treatment" became yet another failed propaganda attempt, foiled by the strength and united efforts of the American spirits long held captive but never broken.

"I was put in several rooms while at Little Vegas," Nat continued. "Morale of the whole camp was about the same, and there was no change really until after the agreement was signed. Then the day came. It was around the first week in March when I was told that I was going home and would be released on the fifth of March. Then on the fourth, everyone was excited because we were the first group to be released from Little Vegas. I didn't sleep much that night. I don't think none of us did. I was given my second good meal, but I still had my doubts. The 'Last Meal,' as they called it, consisted of canned pork, eggs, fried rice, bread and a type of greens, and a small glass of sweetened condensed milk. On the morning of the fifth, Cheese came in and told us we were going home. I had put all the information in my jock strap early that morning. There were thirty-four POWs [chosen to leave] in my group. I was taken out of Little Vegas with the other POWs and taken to a room where we were given new clothes and shoes to wear home."

You carried out information in a jock strap? Nat nodded, "I made a dern jock strap while I was in the jungle in Camp 102. The reason I made it stemmed from them damn boils we got in the jungle camps. My God, I got them all over my groin area, so I made a jock strap. The guards had never taken it from me, so I had it the whole time. I made it out of a leg of them old pajamas, 'cause, you know, they was a mile too long anyway. We got a needle and thread every now and then 'cause if you ripped your pajamas you had to fix them. They told us if they tore up, we wouldn't have no more. One guy had the needle and thread one day, so I ripped that damn leg off the pajamas and made a jock strap out of it."

"It was after being told we were going home that Colonel Guy said that we should carry out all the information that we could. I was chosen to carry the information out in that jock strap. It was all written down on toilet paper [as to] who was in the camps. All the POWs that had died in all the camps that the other POWs had been in and when they had died. We all kept track of the names throughout captivity, but then when we got to Little Vegas and after the Peace Agreement was signed, then we kept it all together. We were able to remember all the men that had died. I brought out every name of everybody that was left, too. It was all the living and dead POWs. There were four that I knew of that had died, and everybody else knew one or two that had died in each group, so there was at least fifteen or twenty of those names. It was a big piece of paper. It was hard to walk!" Nat laughed. "I don't know, though, what they would have done if they had caught me with that," he said quietly, shaking his head.

"Everybody had to undress with the guards watching and then put the clothes on. I had that jock on with all the information in it and was afraid the guards would find it. There's no telling what they would have done if they had. When we started changing, though, Perricone stepped in front of me. I put on that tee shirt first 'cause it was so long, then I pulled the pants on real quick before the guards saw me. Perricone stepped to the side of me so the guards couldn't see anything."

"We all changed and then left Little Vegas. It was really the first time I had walked through the Hilton without being blindfolded. It was great to get the hell out of that camp! I was put on a bus, and we were on our way. We had gone a mile probably when the bus stopped. We were given a beer and were told the same old bull about how good they had been to us. We figured it was over though, 'cause they wouldn't have given you a beer. They was just showing their good attitude and lenient treatment." Nat smirked.

"Well, Billy Beard, he didn't have no control over his kidneys or nothing, but he had a little old journal of a thing that he had to carry, and somebody put a note in his stuff. Well, he had to go to the bathroom, especially after he drunk that beer, and he give it to somebody, and they dumped it. They didn't see it [the note], either, but I had the same information he did. Nobody else carried it out except me. When they took everybody to change clothes, whoever had it gave it to Billy to put it in his little journal thinking it would be a good place to hide it, but the poor old boy couldn't hold onto it. After we drank our beer, then we were taken on to the airport."

"When we got there, on one side they was a big delegation of the Vietnamese. It was mostly high-ranking NVA officers. God, there was Dinks everywhere! The camp commander was there, too. They was having some big deal and all. On the other side was the C-141, and, damn, what a sight that was! We were put in lines of twos and, when our names was called, we stepped over to be greeted by a U.S. officer. We didn't know what to expect 'cause it could have still gone wrong before we got on the plane. There was two guards that went with us, and, by God, I never looked back either! When they called my name, I jumped in that line and never slowed down!"

Nat said, laughing and shaking his head. "I was the first one to be released, and it was hard to believe it was true. As far as I know, I was the first enlisted man that was captured in the south to be released in the north."

"Getting ready to board the plane, we had to go up and do the thing for the Cheese and stand at attention and all. I thought I would just go 'Wham!'" when I went over to him," Nat laughed, thinking about that. "When we crossed the line, I forgot what rank he was, probably a full bird colonel, but, this colonel, though, said, 'By God, we've got you now,' or something to that effect. It was funny, though, what he said. When we crossed that line, we had to salute and all that, then there was another major or colonel standing next to the plane. When we got to the plane, there was either two or three women nurses, but I don't know how many there would be on a crew for a C-141. It was great to see that plane and know that I was going to get on it and come back to the good Ol' USA! It still didn't seem true, though, until the C-141 got airborne."

"I was carrying two bags too, Billy Beards' and mine, 'cause he was real sick and on crutches. He was the second one in our group to get released. I don't know why they didn't take Billy Beard first. I guess it was because they released us according to our date of capture, but I don't know why they didn't put him on first. I was glad to get on first, though. I thought, though, that I would get in that line and have one of my 'dumb' attacks and get up there and bow to the colonel or something!" Nat roared again with laughter. "I think Billy came on, though, right after Flora did. But I carried Billy's bags."

"The first thing, though, was they sat us all down, and, being the first one on, of course I went to the back of the plane. They give us all a pack of cigarettes. The second guy was Carol 'Ed' Flora. He was a Special Forces man captured in late 1966. Me and him went all the way to the back of the plane and lit a cigarette, then, the first thing I knew, Flora told them, 'Hell, he's had five or six heart attacks! Then, my God, them damn nurses took me up there and laid me down on an old stretcher, so I had to ride a damn stretcher all the way to the Philippines with a pressure cuff and all!" Nat laughed while explaining. "So I was put in the very front of the plane on a stretcher 'cause I had had so many heart attacks. At least, that's what they thought I had," his warm grin spreading across his face. "But it didn't' take too long for us to go through the line 'cause there was thirty-four of us, and we were so happy to cross it."

"They gave us coffee or whatever we wanted to drink, then the pilot drove down the runway, and it didn't take but a few minutes, but a lot of things went through our minds. When we got airborne, though, we were gone! The pilot was on there talking to us, but, hell, everyone was so excited I can't remember now what all was said. That was a fun time, though, I'll tell you that!" Nat choked out through the laughter.

"When we got on, they come around and put our rank on us. They either give it to us or pinned it to the coat we had on. Course, they couldn't find mine, so they just give it to me on a piece of paper. The rest, though, had an armband. Hell, I wanted to know what rank I was, too, so I found out I had made Staff Sergeant. See, you went Private, PFC, then Spec 4, and in the infantry then you went to Buck Sergeant then Staff Sergeant and so on," Nat explained.

Did you have an escort of fighters when the C-141 came into Gia Lam airport in Hanoi? "Oh yeah! They had to refuel over there, and they brought the whole damn works and tested that fuel before they put it in our plane. I'm glad they did, my God, there's no telling what could have happened. They brought, I guess it was a chemist, or whoever, but they checked that fuel. They had escorts coming in and going out, too. We saw the plane, though. McNish [a pilot from Nat's hometown] had just left the Philippines when I got there. He was in the first group to go, but I remember we saw the plane coming in. It come right over our camp. It was a C-141."

What did you think when you saw that American plane coming in? "I thought, God, I hope it comes back, 'cause we knew we would be the next ones! We saw it come in and go out, too. Then after that, when the first plane come in, is when they moved four or five of us in that old place that night and told us we would be released the next morning and gave us our big meal. The escorts brought 'em in, though, but they didn't come into the airport. They were far enough out to know what was going on, and then they picked us up again when we got airborne. But when I left for Vietnam, hell, we had all kinds of escorts going into Saigon. They escorted everyone in. I mean, my God, you went in and went straight down! You lost your breath!" Nat laughed. "But leaving Hanoi, just as quick as we got in the air they picked us back up and stayed with us until they got us out of Vietnamese airspace. I don't think it took but about two or two-and-a-half hours to get to the Philippines."

"I weighted around 165 pounds before I was captured. We gained some weight back before we were released. When I got to the Philippines, they weighed everybody and I weighted 128 pounds. I had a twenty-eight inch waist and wore a thirty-four inch coat. I would say I went down, especially after that escape attempt in the jungle, to 115 pounds. I was skin and bones. The darned old pajamas had those old draw strings, and, well, after a while the draw string was so long you could just wrap that dang draw string plumb around and tie it in the back. I don't guess I had over three pair of pajamas the whole time I was there. You wore 'em till they was rags. Two were black, and the other pair was gray with red stripes. It got to where when you washed 'em, you couldn't scrub 'em. Course, we didn't have that much soap to wash 'em in, anyway, so we just rinsed 'em out. In the rooms, though, we never wore 'em. We just wore those shorts and a shirt. The only time, really, when we put them on was when it got cold or when we had to go see the Cheese. When you went to see him, you had to put the whole set of pajamas on-- out of respect I guess."

"I was in prison five years, eight months, and nineteen days '*for the convenience of the government*'-- 2,094 days. It was a long, damn time, I know that." Nat paused for a moment, then continued with these thoughts: "The guys I was captured with... We are still like brothers. After living with each other for almost six years, the five of us grew very close in the time that we were together. A bond was formed between us that will never be broken. We have probably told each other things that we would not tell anyone else. We didn't have nothing but each other. We had already lost everything, but especially our freedom. When you lose everything like we did, you really get close with the ones around you. We have a bond that will never be broken."

Chapter 15

"Mother, I'm Home!"

The strain of the morning was beginning to wear on us both. As Mrs. Henry and I sat at the small kitchen table, I knew my next few questions would be as difficult, if not more so, than all the others combined. We had both shared reliving the most horrible days a mother could imagine, short of actually learning her child was dead, but the thoughts of Nat's homecoming, although joyful, were almost more than Mrs. Henry could put into words.

When did you learn that Nat was finally going to come home? "I think it was the fourth of March when we first realized that he was gonna get released," she began. "Major Pritchard called me that day in January.... I forget what day it was.... Oh, I believe it was January 28th of '73," she recalled, after thinking for a minute. That's when they notified us that they had a list with his name on it. But, anyway, Major Pritchard said they was gonna release some names, then said, 'I will call you as soon as I know,' and I said, 'Well, good.' But that night, he was knocking on our door. He had brought the word! He come up and said, 'I left [the base], and I never got a penny! I ain't got no money, and I done run out of gas!' And, you know, I never thought once about giving him some money. I don't know how he ever got back!" she said, laughing hard. "He was coming from Dalhonega, Georgia."

The moment Major Pritchard learned that Nat's name was on the release list, he wanted to go immediately to the small town in North Carolina and relate the wonderful news to the family of which he had become so close. Without thought for his own well being, Major Pritchard left his post in Georgia with only the uniform on his back. This unplanned response by the Henry family support officer simply exemplifies the dedication and devotion these men had to their charges. To this day, from amid all the excitement and confusion of that night long ago, Mrs. Henry still has no idea how the young officer managed to get back home.

"Boyd Holbrooks. [our neighbor] come down the road the next morning. I don't know what I was a doing, baking I think, but anyway, he stopped and said, 'I knew you had somebody here last night, and I just thought it might have been your 'officer,' because I seen where he pulled out on the side of the road!'" Mrs. Henry laughed again, remembering the fiasco of the night before.

"Then Major Pritchard called me one morning at four o'clock. He said, 'Get up and turn on the television!' I said, 'Now what's the matter?' and he said, 'You're going to get to see Nat!'" Mrs. Henry caught her throat and choked back the tears, then swallowed hard a couple times before continuing. "He was being taken off the plane in the Philippines." And that was the first time you got to see him? She was once again trying to stop the flow of tears, but this time they were tears of joy and relief. Nodding her head 'yes,' she continued relating the emotional story. "Thurman and I stayed around here the next morning for a little while, then he said, 'Well, I'll go to work.' Of course, he was so excited he couldn't work, so it wasn't long before they [her husband and son Harry] came back," she laughed slightly. "I was on the telephone 'cause everybody was calling from around here, and then all at once the phone went dead. Then a man spoke on the phone and said, 'This is John Smith, and we've cleared all the lines for you 'cause you're getting a long distance call.'" Sleepless nights filled with fear and uncertainty were now coming to an end for Nat's mother and family, as she held her breath waiting for the first sound from her youngest son.

My throat choked with hers as tears mixed with laughter when Mrs. Henry recalled that glorious morning at 9:15 when she heard her son's voice on the phone after almost six years. "I can't express how I felt," she replied, when asked what her thoughts were at that moment. Mrs. Henry again grasped her throat, trying to talk through the constricting lump that was making speech difficult. Tears were streaming down my face, as well, as I imagined how she must have felt hearing the lost voice of a son she loved dearly and had feared dead for so many years.

For a few moments we both sat silent during a time when no words could be spoken and when none were needed. After trying to wipe the continuous flow of tears, we both laughed at our flood of emotions, then tried to continue with the conversation. "He said he would be home soon," she said, wiping her eyes once more, "but he didn't know just when. Thurman and Harry got to talk to him, too, but I don't remember how long we talked. He just asked about everybody and everything and said he was all right. Then I talked to his escort, SFC Hyman. He called and talked and said, 'He's all right, but that he takes a bath every few minutes!' He said, 'Every time I turn around, he's in the shower. Then in a few minutes, he's back in the tub!' He said, 'He's the cleanest thing, 'cause he's sure taking his baths!'" We both laughed heartily at the thought of Nat endlessly scrubbing his body, while trying to remove six years of dirt, grime, and painful memories he had acquired while being held captive within the stinking prison cells and cages of Vietnam.

What happened after you received the phone call? "We were taken to Augusta, Georgia," she said, "and Major Pritchard had took us out to supper. We had to go with him to the Officer's Club, and while we was eating he got paged. Then he come back and said, 'You keep my stuff here, 'cause I've got to go make a phone call.' Well, I held onto everything he had, so he went and made the phone call, and then he come back and said, 'We're gonna have to go! They're waiting for us at the motel to go to the airport!' So when we got back to the motel, he kept waiting and waiting and so I said, 'Well let's go! You was in such a hurry, so *now* what's the matter?'" Mrs. Henry laughed and said, "You know, I talked to him just like I would to one of my own! But we always had a good time." We both laughed at the manner in which she addressed the escort, then once again she continued with her story. "Then Major Pritchard said, 'We'll go in a few minutes.' Then he kept a-waiting, and I was wondering what was wrong when somebody knocked on the door. He opened it right quick, and it was the florist with a big bouquet for me from President Nixon!" she exclaimed as a wide grin was spreading across her face. "That's what he was waiting on!"

"Then we got in a motorcade after that. There was eighteen motorcycles that led us, and I don't know *how* many was behind us, and then they took us off to the airport. We had the VIP treatment, though. Then we went into a place in the airport to sit down and it was full [of people], but, you know, in just a few minutes everybody was out of there! They made everybody leave so we could be alone. We sat there and Major Pritchard sat on the floor beside me. Then he got another page to go to the phone, so when he came back he said he'd been talking to Nat's escort, Mr. Hyman. He said Nat was nervous 'cause he knew he was coming in. They was both talking to him and to the escort."

"We went outside, then in just a little while this big jet come in. They rolled out the red carpet for him to walk down. There was a lot of people there, but they had it roped off," she said. Then I asked, "So who got the first hug? I bet you did!" Mrs. Henry laughed, "Well, no, there was a little girl on the sidelines that was jumping up and down, and she run to him first. She was somebody from Augusta and had his [POW] bracelet, and she just had to hug him! She was about ten or eleven years old, I guess. I got my hug, though!" Mrs. Henry exclaimed, then started laughing.

"After that, we went back to the motel. We had a room, he had a room, and they had two more rooms reserved for Harry and his wife Mary Ann. They had just got married while we were down there. Then Pratt and Cora, his wife, and their little girl Tricia was in one room. She was just three years old, and she had a birthday while we was there, too, and, oh, they had her a big cake! She would come and smile at them big black Sergeants, and, you know, they would grab her up and carry her all over the place! She would ask them, 'You gonna take me on the 'T-Bus?'" And that would just tickle them to death! After we come back home the escort, SSgt. Hyman, came up here and said, 'You know, she named it the 'T-Bus,' 'cause everybody calls it the 'T-Bus' now. It was one of those smaller buses that took us everywhere, like these shuttle buses. To her it looked like a school bus, though," Mrs. Henry said through her laughter.

"They treated us real good, though," she continued. "We stayed there maybe three days, then we come on home, and Nat come back at the end of the week. Well, they were going through all these tests and everything, medical tests, and, of course, they was debriefing him, because they said he could give them names and serial numbers of people that died in the camps he was in. They said it was amazing he could remember that much."

What was the first meal Nat wanted you to cook for him? "Let's see," she said, trying to recall. "They come in that night, and I had cooked supper, but they had eat in town before they come on down here to the house. Then the next day, I had baked ham, bean salad... just everything!" she said with a loving chuckle. "I don't know what all I *did* cook! But I remember his escort thought that was the best meal he had ever eat!" We both laughed again as Mrs. Henry remembered all the food the two men devoured. "It was continual cooking when he was around," she said. "I fixed cornbread and hot rolls. I was always making homemade rolls. Danny O' Daniels was the escort that come home with him. He was waiting at Fort Gordon and was the one that brought Nat home. Hyman, the one that come in on the plane with him, left and went back to wherever it was he was stationed, but years later he came back to see Nat."

I was curious as to how the town home-folks had greeted their newly released war hero, and proceeded to ask Mrs. Henry about it. "Well, the buildings was just loaded with people," she said. "I'll tell you, though, I never was so tired, a-cooking for so many and doing everything. So many people wanted to come down and talk to him, but he never liked to talk about it 'cause he would have nightmares after that." Mrs. Henry paused for a moment, then stared out the kitchen window as if in deep thought. "They went on a long time," she said softly. "I used to go into him and talk to him, and I reckon my voice would kinda make him wake up. One night he was beating the wall with his fist, and I went in and asked him what's the matter. And, of course, after a while he talked and he said, 'Snakes.' He talked about how they would crawl on them. But I would always try to steer away from anything about over there."

Mrs. Henry and I had moved out onto the front porch and sat in rocking chairs while sifting through an old suitcase full of official documents she had received while Nat was a Prisoner of War. She had saved almost everything, and although silverfish scurried amongst the papers, there was a goldmine of information just waiting to be discovered. We looked at documents from President Nixon, General William Westmoreland, and numerous other prominent figures who expressed concern and sent their blessings for the safe return of the POWs. While reading a letter from then President Nixon, Mrs. Henry commented, "You know, people can say whatever they want about Nixon, but to me, he'll always be a great man." She paused momentarily, then continued with her thoughts. "They talk about [how bad] the CIA was and all, but you know, when there was a bunch coming in to bomb, the CIA would arm the POWs with a song like 'Ghost Riders In The Sky,' and then they would know to take cover. Some of the POWs would whistle the tune to let the others know. Nat said you would just be going along and wouldn't really see anyone, but then you'd hear that song. It was usually someone whistling it. I remember him telling me also that before they got to leave, they were all sitting around one night and said they heard the song 'The Red River Valley-- From This Valley They Say You Are Leaving,' from the group that was leaving the camps. He said they knew then that they were gonna be released. He said you would never see anybody, but you would hear 'em. They were always whistling those songs when they would hear planes coming over the camp."

"I remember he said when he was in the jungle in Cambodia, he would hear the wild roosters crow and they [the Vietnamese] had this suspicion [belief] that whoever heard the first crow, then there would be a death in their family. He told me later, 'Mother, I heard it in '68 and heard the rooster crow *after* midnight, did anyone die?' I said 'Yeah, Harry, my brother died. It sure makes you wonder, don't it?"

"There was so much we talked about, but I remember it wasn't too long after he came home that he was looking over there in that drawer and said, 'Mother, where did you get this address?' I said, 'Well, that's where I sent your packages to all the time.' Then he looked at me and said, 'It was just across the street!'" Mrs. Henry added with a sigh in her voice, "All that time and he never got the first one."

Chapter 16

Free Soil at Last

"There were crowds of people at Clark when we got there. We got off the plane according to rank, though, instead of by date of capture. Leopold was the highest rank in our group, so he got off first. He had to make a speech before we could get on off, then we filed off and went through the line, then they put us on another bus and took us on to the hospital. There was a lot of people, though, at the airfield. That's when they had a lot of troops stationed there, too."

"The first thing they did when they got us to the hospital was feed us. The first thing I had was a bunch of sweets. Then I remember getting a milkshake, a coke, and a beer!" We both started laughing at the combination of beverages. "I drunk all three of 'em, too!" he exclaimed through the laughter. "When we got there, they, hell... We didn't know they would give us a beer, so we got the milkshake and all, and that's when we met the escort. Then Sgt. Hyman, my escort, asked if we wanted a beer, so that's when I got a beer, too! It's a wonder we didn't get the stomachache, but we did get dysentery and diarrhea the next morning!" Nat followed that statement with even more happy laughter. "It was worth it, though. That was about three o'clock in the afternoon, I guess, then everybody went back and had steak and eggs about eight o'clock that night. After that, we went to our rooms, and that's when the escorts came and debriefed us for a bit. They told us if our family was still living or dead and some of the things that had happened, then we called home. After that we went and ate the 'big meal.' I had steak and potatoes and rolls and milk, and then I had coffee." A slight pause slipped into the conversation, then Nat stated cautiously, "I didn't drink a beer with supper." After that comment we both erupted in laughter again."

"After we eat, we went to the PX. The first thing I bought was a Zippo lighter! I bought a Zippo lighter, a camera, candy, and I didn't buy no clothes or nothing, but I got two Mounds bars, and chewing gum, I think. Of course, we got cigarettes, 'cause we all smoked then, and I think everybody bought a Zippo lighter!" Nat laughed hard again, remembering the importance of buying that Zippo lighter. "I remember at one of our reunions after we got home years later, old Frank had given his lighter to his daddy. He said later that when his dad died that he got his lighter back and still has it. I don't know if I've still got mine or not. If I do, I don't know where it would be."

"The next day we went and got fitted for our new uniforms, and they give us another haircut. Tom Horio and I had cut each other's hair about a week before we had left there. Course they had to cut it again, so I had a darn crew cut. So we went through all the debriefing and all, and they asked all the same questions, who all was there, course it was all on that information I had carried out. They just hit the high spots, though, but after I got to Fort Gordon, we went through two weeks of it down there. Nothing but debriefing. They had a lot of pictures of guys, and we had to go through and see if we could pick anyone out. I knew several of them. The hardest ones to pick out, though, was the four of us!" he said laughing and shaking his head. "I don't know why that was so hard, but I guess you're just not thinking of yourself. I went through that thing, though, and picked out what I could, then that officer said, 'Let's go back through it.' So we went back through it again, and I got on a page, and he said, 'Do you not know none of them?' and I said, 'Good God, that's the four of us!' I'll never forget that," Nat laughed. "But, you know, it's just in your mind, you know, that you're looking for some of the other guys, and I just passed over myself and the others. But, see, I was the only one at Fort Gordon. Part of 'em were in Texas, and part of 'em went to Fort Mammoth in New Jersey. That's where

I think Frank and Perricone went. We had all been separated by then, but I went through that book and missed the whole bunch of us," he said and chuckled once more.

Phase I of Operation Homecoming was to get the POWs out of Vietnam as quickly as possible. Once the men reached Clark Air Force Base in the Philippines, Phase II began, which entailed a quick but thorough debriefing. The Joint Debriefing and Casualty Reporting Center, (JDCRC) under the direction of CINCPAC, conducted this process. JDCRC had representatives from each military service. Civilian and foreign returnees were debriefed by the service with whom they were associated or by members of the U.S. Embassy, Manila. Each service handled its own debriefings, differing in approach, but following common debriefing instructions. The Army and Marine Corps used professional intelligence debriefers whose sole job was debriefing. The Navy and Air Force used a combination of escort and debriefer, with the Navy using only Air Intelligence officers.

What was the role of the escorts that were assigned to you? "Hell, they was our servants!" Nat said with a laugh. "I mean, they did all we wanted. No, really, they knew the base and all, and, like Hyman, he knew what all was going on, so he took me as far as Fort Gordon. Then I got with O' Daniels. He carried the records that I needed and took me to the places for all the tests. They furnished the car and driver, and me and the escort rode in the back. Hell, we was uptown!" Nat exclaimed with a chuckle. "We got close, too. I talked to Hyman just about three or four months ago. He lives in Fayetteville now. He stayed in service I believe twenty-six years, and quick as he got out, he went right back into Civil Service. I think he's got about six months left to retire. I know when we got home they'd answer the phone, too, if somebody called. They didn't know who all was trying to call, and they didn't want us saying too much, anyway, so they screened all our phone calls."

What was your treatment like at Clark Air Force Base? "It was great. We had the run of the place. After arriving at Clark, everyone was assigned a military escort. The guy I had was SFC Sterling Hyman. We were given all we wanted and what we wanted for dinner that night. We sure went through the food!" Nat laughed, remembering that evening. "I called home that night and talked to my parents. It was great to hear their voice after almost six years and not knowing if they were dead or alive."

"The first night, I know we got to the Philippines, they had us four to the room. It was Perricone, Frank, me, and I think it was McFail. But nobody slept that night. I can't remember, but I was trying to remember how many pounds of meat and eggs we went through that first night, but my God, it was a big number! Most of us eat scrambled eggs, but I forget how many dozens they said they went through, but it was a bunch of 'em! The next morning for breakfast we had eggs and bacon, toast, biscuits.... Hell, we tried some of all of it!"

"We was so excited though we couldn't sleep. Then after we went and got them Zippo lighters, we got cokes and smoked cigarettes all night!" Once again, the laughter broke out between the two of us. Nat's wife Becky was at the kitchen table sewing and laughing just as hard at our conversation. "I got Winstons," he continued, "'cause that was what I smoked before I got captured." Nat grinned with a far away look in his eye, then stated nonchalantly, "A Zippo lighter, a carton of Winstons, and candy bars," then started laughing all over again.

During our conversation, Nat took out an old photo album, which contained numerous pictures and newspaper clippings. He flipped to the middle and showed me an eight by ten black and white photograph of the thirty-four men that had just been released from the prisons in North Vietnam. We looked at the group photo after the men had arrived and were settled in the Philippines, then Nat pointed out the men he had spent most of his time with. "The guys I was captured with.....We are still like brothers. We have a bond that will never be broken."

Dressed in pajamas, robes, and slippers, the men in the photo seemed to stare back at me with a haunting expression as I carefully studied each face. Hollow, sunken eyes, darkened with torture and time, seemed even more recessed amid the gaunt faces in which they rested. Faces that belonged to the once carefree men, most still in their mid to late twenties, now reflected that of much older men who had seen and endured a hundred lifetimes of pain and debilitating torture. Bodies, who just a few years before, were sleek, muscular, and in prime physical condition, were now held together by skin,

139

bones, and the sheer will and determination to survive.

Sitting comfortably in oversized chairs and sofas while posing for the photograph, the men looked happy and content. There was something that touched me about that picture, though. The smiles were soft and warm. The men were clean and well-fed, as they spent the night in the Philippines on free soil. But beyond the façade of cleanliness and gentle smiles, a different message cried out from the old photograph. *'I have done my duty to my country because I wanted to... not because I had to. I have been to hell and beyond within the prisons of Vietnam and came back for more. I have endured more than any human should ever endure. I faced and fought with the devil, and I won. I am now on free soil, and to be able to speak those words, makes the past a burden I proudly bear.'*

There was a glow about that picture that was hard to describe. It wasn't from the smiling faces or the clean clothes the men wore. It didn't come from the expertise of the photographer or the lighting in the room. The iron will and soul of each of the thirty-four men who had fought for their lives on a daily basis and had won generated that glow. It came from a collective defiant attitude that could not be beaten by even the most inhumane enemy. It was..... the glow of Freedom!

"I stayed at Clark for a couple of days, where we were debriefed and checked by the doctors. We were issued new uniforms for our trip back home. After that, we boarded planes headed for home. We stopped in Hawaii first, then on to Texas, then Pensacola, Florida. Me and John Deering were the last two on the plane. We flew together from Texas to Florida, where he got off. It was kinda funny 'cause John looked at me and said, 'We got this whole big plane all to ourselves.'" Nat laughed. "After Deering got off, it was just me on my way to Fort Gordon, Georgia. All the places that we landed on the way home, we all got a great reception. At every stop, we were given a great welcome. It was a good feeling for us to see that the American people were showing us so much support. I got there [to Fort Gordon] around eight o'clock the evening of March eighth. It was hard to believe that the six years of hell was now over, and I was back on the Ol' USA soil! My parents were there waiting for my arrival, and it was great to see them."

"After arriving at Fort Gordon, SFC Hyman left, and I was assigned another [military] escort. He was SSgt Danny O'

Daniels. The escort stayed with us all the time and was involved in the debriefing. I went through a lot of debriefing and medical evaluations while at Fort Gordon. When we came home, we got a pass. I came home that weekend, then went back 'cause I stayed at Fort Gordon three months. I landed on the eighth of March, and stayed in the Philippines three days, then I stayed at Fort Gordon until they discharged me on August the eighth. Really, I stayed there five months, but I had two thirty-day leaves when I came home, then went right back and went through the same tests again. I stayed there about two weeks, I guess, before I came home. They let me come in that one weekend 'cause we was going through all them tests and all, but they were having a parade and all here at home for me, so they let me come in for that. But I had to check back into the base at 8:00 Sunday night. They just let us have the weekend, and that was it. They checked everything from the top of your head to your toes and over again. We had x-rays, EKG's, and everything. When they finally figured out I was having seizures, I had to go through two or three EG&G's. Then we went and had all our teeth fixed, but it was a damn physical! I changed uniforms I think three times within three months. I went from a twenty-eight waist to a thirty-two. Actually it was ninety days of convalescent leave, but we didn't get it all at one time, we had to spread it out."

What did you want to do your first weekend home? "At the end of that weekend, I just wanted to go around and see the people I knew. Most of the older people that lived in this community, though, that I knew had already died. I'll never forget, though, old man Joe Daves, he lived to be ninety-nine or so. I guess he was close to ninety or ninety-one then, but that old man recognized me when we landed in the Philippines," Nat said with a thoughtful smile.

What was the parade like that was given in your honor? "It was great! We definitely noticed that Franklin had grown! I believe they said there was like five thousand people that turned out for the parade. We were all on Main Street and had all these banners that said 'Welcome Home Nat and Tommy.' They even had things strung over here at the Burningtown Church. Some guys that worked for the power company had run it from power pole to power pole. It was all the way across the road! All the roads and houses were covered in signs and flags!" Nat exclaimed and laughed. "When I got to the

Philippines, they said there was another guy there from Franklin, North Carolina, and I said, 'Surely to hell not!' I didn't know he was even captured until I got to Clark. That was the first time I knew he was even there [in Vietnam]. That was really weird, though, with as small a town as Franklin to have two captured out of it. Once we got home, we didn't see each other much, though. He was a pilot and they seemed to have their version and we [enlisted men] had our version, so we didn't compare notes much."

"I'll never forget, though, when we come home for that parade, O' Daniels and I came in, and they told us to come to the Chamber of Commerce. Well, when I left, the Chamber of Commerce was that old building up on the square, and when I got up there, I couldn't find it. So I stopped and asked somebody, I can't remember who, but he said, 'They, my God, it's out there on the Georgia road past the school on the right.' When we got out there, we seen it, but things were so different when I was here before. When I left, the old courthouse was still here and Dixie Hall— one of the most beautiful buildings in town. I mean there was definitely some change though."

What was the "Freedom Tree" you mentioned earlier? Nat started laughing. "The Freedom Tree was a Christmas tree! Wilfred Corbin was the one that give me the tree, but when I come home there was this Christmas tree in my bedroom! It was all decorated in red, white, and blue ribbons and ornaments with tons of packages under it also wrapped in patriotic colors. I got some of the darndest presents, though. All kinds of cologne, clothes, bunches of billfolds, a couple electric razors, just a ton of stuff. First Union Bank gave me this pewter platter with the Great Seal on it. It was funny, though, having Christmas in March!" he said with a laugh. "Ford Motor Company gave us all a car, too. Mine was a '73 LTD."

What were some of the things you wanted to do when you got back home? "Have a good time!" We both laughed at the simplicity and immediate response of Nat's answer. "I wanted to enjoy life, party, and do a lot of fishing. I used to love to go fishing. I guess, the first leave I come home on I went fishing. I know a lot of 'em came home and drank like a fish and all. Course I had my beer and all, but life's too short to spend it that way."

Chapter 17

The Quiet Life

"I stayed at Fort Gordon until August of '73, when I was given a medical retirement for a permanent disability. After I got out, I just enjoyed life for a couple of months. In October, I went into the construction business and had a backhoe and dump truck. I was in this for about eighteen months, but had to get out for health reasons. I would have been in it now if I was able to do it. After I got out of construction, though, I was bored, so I went back to school and took horticulture at Haywood Community College. It was hard to go back since I had been out of school for seven years, and I was older than my teachers, but I am glad I went and finished the eighteen month course."

"I tried to find my good friend Paul Daves when I got back home. We had gone all through boot camp together and were even together for a while in Vietnam. He knew I was from Franklin, but I found out later that he couldn't remember my Mama and Daddy's names, and, Lord, I couldn't remember his, either. I just remembered he lived in Knoxville, and every time Becky and I got anywhere near there we started calling and trying to find him. We didn't think to check on the outskirts of Knoxville though, but we called three or four Paul Daves in that area trying to find him." Nat chuckled then recalled, "I remember one time I called one number and asked if this was Paul Daves, and he said yes it was. Then I asked him when was he in

Vietnam and he laughed and said, 'Hell, I was in World War II!'"

"In 1994 Paul called one night out of the blue. Becky and I had gone somewhere that night, and when we came home there was a message on the answering machine. He said, 'If this is the Nat Henry I went to Vietnam with in 1966, please call, and if not, I'm sorry I've got the wrong number.' Hell, it was like talking to the dead! After talking for a while we decided it had been about twenty-five years since we had seen each other, and he had been trying to find me all that time, too." Nat stated. "We called them right away, and Paul and his wife Karen said they had gone to see the Vietnam Memorial's *Moving Wall* when it was in Knoxville to see if my name was on it. He knew I was from Franklin, and when they realized my name wasn't there, they just started trying to find my number." Becky added to the conversation, "We talk all the time now and get together at least two or three times a year and go out to eat. Right after we got in touch with each other, we went over there to meet them. We were so excited we forgot to tell them what kind of car we would be driving or what color it was, so we ended up driving around and around that damn parking lot! I told Nat that we should have told them we would be driving a green car but we didn't." Nat and Becky both laughed remembering that night. "Paul works for Hackney now and has for years. He spent his tour in Vietnam and came back to Fort Campbell for his remaining four months, then started working at Hackney Foods and has been there ever since."

"There was this one guy, too, named Eddie Moody from Waynesville. Becky and I had stayed up one night with a sick friend and just come home and got in the bed when my daughter-in-law called and woke us up. She said John, our son, was wanting my truck or something, and I was so tired I blessed her out. Then I just got on up and made a pot of coffee. Then the phone rang again, and I was ready to snap their head off, too! The man on the phone asked what was I doing, and I said I was trying to get some sleep about thirty minutes ago, but I'm up now. He said his name was Eddie Moody and that he did backhoe work in Waynesville. It took me a minute to figure out who he was, but he had been in our unit and ended up making it back okay after that battle at Pleiku. I tried calling him several times after that but never could get in touch with him. I ran into him, too, when I was going to school at Haywood Tech not long after I had come back home. He said he had some good pictures of when we were there, but I haven't been able to talk to him since."

How did you and Becky meet? "Blind date!" Becky exclaimed with a laugh. "Oh Lord," Nat chimed in with a light blush and a little-boy grin on his face. "I was living in Waynesville while in school and met Becky in 1975. It was me and Danny Reynolds. We went down to her folk's place to blowup a stump. I don't know what happened that day, but we never did get that stump to blowup. We used about three sticks of dynamite, but it never would blow! We tied the sticks of dynamite together and ran the wires to the battery of an old truck to set it off." Nat laughed while shaking his head, "Since we couldn't get that stump out, we decided to take Becky and go to town and put soapsuds in the town fountain. There were so many cops, though, we never did get to do that!"

"We dated for almost two years, though, then we were married on May 28, 1976. We moved back to Franklin after I got out of school and bought some property that had been my granddad's old place. We dated when John, our son, was still real little. We'd fix a hot dog and a coke for him, then he would eat that and sleep the rest of the night," Becky added. "He was six when we got married, then I adopted him." Nat recalled. "I sure don't want to go back and relive those days, though," Becky exclaimed through her laughter. "It was enough to give you more than a few gray hairs! We've been married now twenty-three years in May if I don't beat him to death before then." We all laughed at the good-natured teasing, then it erupted once again when Nat added, "I told them I was like a cat and had nine lives, but, hell, evidently I've already lived seven or eight of 'em!"

"We built a house and started a business right after we moved back to Franklin," Nat recalled. "I started out with one greenhouse for the first year, but we kept expanding and soon had a thriving business. We were in business for twenty-one years and called it 'Henry's Greenhouses.' We both enjoyed it, although it was a lot of work. It was like dairy farming... Seven days a week, 365 days a year. We closed it last year, but it gets in your blood, and we still miss it. But we're also glad we are not in it no longer."

"I spend much of my time now doing my yard work and raising a garden. I lost my dad last October 1997, so I try to keep up his place also. After he died, I kept his cattle, too, so I also take care of them. I put up my hay in summer, so it has just become a hobby, but I enjoy it. Becky does crafts as a hobby, also. We have one son, John, and one granddaughter. Life has been good to me since I came home, and I have definitely enjoyed it."

"It's September now and just about time for fall. This time of the year the sky gets so blue it still reminds me of the skies over there. One of my favorite hobbies is hunting ginseng, and this is the only time of the year it can be dug. I will go way back in the mountains and hunt and just enjoy the freedom of being able to get out and do what I want. I thank the Good Lord everyday for being able to get up and do what I want to do. I know what the word 'freedom' means and how much it means to me 'cause I've been on the other side of it."

"Most American people don't know what it means to have their freedom. It is just something that we don't realize how valuable it is until it is gone. I know there was a lot of things that went on in Vietnam that the American people will probably never know. I knew one thing, though... The day I was captured, the battle report was not right. There was a lot of stuff that was covered up. The Vietnam War was a very unpopular war, and the American people didn't support the war or its troops. In Vietnam, the American youth was put to the test and came out courageous men. The majority of the troops were only teenagers... But all wars are hell, as Vietnam proved. The people of America did show a lot of support for the POWs and their families, though. I know when I came home, I got POW bracelets from a lot of people, and it means a lot to me to know we had that much support."

"If it had not been for the Lord above, I probably would have never made it home. There are three things that I think all of the American people should remember and they are: 1) Never lose faith in God; 2) never lose faith in your fellow man; and 3) always have faith and trust in your country. It really takes a person losing their freedom to truly appreciate it, because we don't really appreciate the true meaning of the word 'freedom.'"

For his time as a soldier and a POW during the Vietnam conflict, SSgt. Nathan Henry received the following citations:

- **The Silver Star** - For Gallantry in Action in Southeast Asia - November 1967

- **The Bronze Star** - For Meritorious Achievement in Ground Operations Against Hostile Forces in Vietnam - October 1971 to May 1972
- **The Bronze Star** - First Oak Leaf Cluster - For Meritorious Achievement in Ground Operations Against Hostile Forces in Southeast Asia - July 12, 1967 to March 5, 1973
- **Purple Heart** - For Wounds Received in Action in Vietnam - July 1967
- **Purple Heart** - First Oak Leaf Cluster - For Wounds Received in Action and Maltreatment During Captivity in Vietnam - July 12, 1967 to March 5, 1973

Nat Henry delivered the following speech during a Veteran's Day celebration at a local Community College not long after he returned to the United States as a free man. I felt it was necessary to show his thoughts at that time reflect the same way he feels today about the country for which he gave up almost six years of his life. It is reprinted from the actual hand-written document Mr. Henry used that Veteran's Day so many years ago:

"I am pleased to be asked to come here today and try to speak. I think this is a very good thing that the school is doing in honoring the veterans on Veteran's Day. I am proud to be able to stand here before you today and say that I am a veteran. We Americans tend to forget the veteran a lot of times, but I believe the American people are becoming more aware of who the veteran is and what he has done for this great country we live in today. I think that all veterans deserve being recognized, especially the Vietnam veteran. I am proud to say that I am a Vietnam veteran and not some draft dodger who ran off to Canada when he received the call to defend and fight for his country. In Vietnam, the American youth was put to the test. The average fighting man was really just a boy out of high school, but we stood proud and tall and fought courageously. In Vietnam, boys turned into men overnight. We had no choice, even though we were fighting a losing war half-way around the world. You can't win a war that the politician and government is trying to fight in Washington. That war should have been won in less than a year, but, like I say, it was a political war. It was an unpopular war, but we got the call to go, and we went and stood proud and tall. But even today, the Vietnam veteran is looked down on to a certain degree. But most of us are just average

Americans like the rest of you. What worries me is if we get into another war, are the American boys going to go and fight? Look at the draft dodgers who went to Canada. After the war was over, they were allowed to come back. What impact is this going to have on these men? Believe me, America lost a lot of its pride when this happened.

"I was held a POW for nearly six years. The first two and a half years I spent in the jungles of Cambodia. I was captured on July 12, 1967. I escaped on November 6 of '67. In the jungle they had wood stocks where they would put one leg in them at night. After the escape attempt, they put both legs in them for seven months, twenty-four hours a day. They cut our food in half, and we got a bowl of rice and some rock salt each day. A person didn't realize how much freedom means until he loses it. I spent six Christmases in prison, but the first was the saddest. They played Christmas carols in the distance so we could barely hear them. But a person can take more in a situation like that than he realizes he can. In November of 1969, they moved us north to Hanoi. We walked for forty-eight days and road trucks for three or four days. We arrived at a camp outside Hanoi on Christmas Day of 1969. They tried to keep our morale as low as possible all of the time. But after we got in Hanoi, the food was better, but we were put in a camp with the rooms painted black and no windows. I stayed in this camp for thirteen months. We never got to go outside except once a week for a bath.

"I was listed as an MIA until the Peace Agreement was signed in January of 1973. My family never knew anything or that I was even a prisoner until the Peace Agreement was signed. I was never allowed to write or receive mail. I have all the respect in the world for the pilots who were captured in the north. I am not saying our treatment was worse than theirs, but it wasn't any better, either. I know the pilots did get to receive some mail and packages, and the ones who were captured in the south and held in the north didn't get to write or receive mail. My family wrote and sent packages during the whole six years, but I never received none.

"Life means a lot more to me now. I appreciate the smaller things such as soap, hot water, good food, shoes, and I could go on. The American people take for granted the good life we have here in the United States. We have all seen rough times at one time or another, but it is nothing compared to what the people in a communist country have each day. I hope we never see *another war, but if we do, I say to you young people, go on and serve your country and be proud of it because tomorrow you will be the leaders of our great nation.*

"When we escaped, they told us when the war was over we would be held and tried as war criminals, but they let us go. As for recovering the bodies, they will never get them all because, like the men who died in the jungle, they never marked any graves. I would like to leave three thoughts with you. First, never lose faith in God. Second, never lose faith in your country, and third, but not least, never lose faith in your fellow man. Today is a day to remember all the veterans of all the wars and also a special group of veterans who have a lot in common. We are the POWs. But, most important, let's not forget all those who made the supreme sacrifice and gave their lives so we could and can enjoy the freedom like we have today. May God bless all of you."

Today Nat and Becky live a quiet life in the safe serenity of the Blue Ridge Mountains of North Carolina. Life is really no different for them than other families, except maybe they've had a few more sleepless nights, a few more nightmares than some might have had, or possibly a memory that makes the current reality a blessing. For the most part, however, they cherish their grandchild, welcome visits from friends and family, and simply live life to its fullest. But then, isn't that what sacrifice is all about?

Chapter 18

Final Thoughts

Rice paddies low and flat cross-stitched the open fields, then crept slowly from their trenches up to the feet of sprawling mountain ranges. Along this path forming thick stands of bamboo, straight jointed stalks in varying shades of green rose to several feet above the ground, growing six to eight inches in diameter and providing a natural barrier to intruders upon the land. Footbridges often consisted of three or four poles of this bamboo lashed together with hemp vine and placed precariously across dangerous churning waters.

Penetrating further still into the murky green, tendrillar vines hung as rippled curtains blocking all light and sense of direction. Their long, entangled arms wrapped around the bodies of our men as if trying to hold their prey captive deep within the bowels of darkness. Broad-leafed palms could provide cool shade on a hot day, or hide a body that would never be seen again. Yet small spears of sunshine pierced the heavy green canopy, sporadically providing a kaleidoscope of light, and proving, yet again, that somewhere above there is a God in heaven watching over those who tread below.

Deeper still, a fog slithered quietly through the tangle of undergrowth and scrub brush, creating a ghostly film that hung deathly silent amid the forests' inhabitants. Rising from the many streams and rivers that snaked through the jungle, then heated by the tropical sun, the white smothering veil of fog seemed to cloak everything with a shroud of impending death. Once the rains came, it was even worse, because it didn't just rain in Vietnam— it poured. Torrents of rain. Cold, bone-chilling rain that worked its way into the deepest darkest crevices of everything that dared to penetrate its borders. There was no escape.

There was no escape for the land either. Ravaged by war, the face of Vietnam became distorted and scarred forever. Both sides destroyed villages and hamlets. Crops and lush vegetation of bygone days flourished, but was soon annihilated by fires and napalm, then left to wither and die under the oppressive rays of a broiling sun. Bomb craters patterned the ground like huge drops of rain upon a previously still pond, while trees, barren and broken by the blasts, now stand scattered among the once tropical beauty of a life-producing forest.

Many years will pass before the emerald greens return again to the ancient lands of Vietnam and remove the visual scars of war. But, then again, how many years will pass before our men can remove their own scars that are so deeply embedded in their minds and hearts? How many years will it take for the pain and horror of sleepless nights to give way to peaceful slumber?

At times I sit motionless and stare from the security of a tree line into the quiet green of a forest. On occasion, a bird will light upon a branch, survey its surroundings, then take to wing and disappear into the black of the woods beyond. As I look still deeper into the ever-thickening trees, the quiet green becomes a screaming black, and my mind begins to wonder. It is here that I know I can walk without fear. Without the threat of "Charlie," or booby traps, or pungi stakes. It is here that I need not fear for my safety or for the destruction of my home and those I love. It is also here that I can't help but imagine what our captured servicemen must have thought as they walked precariously and under great force through the greens of the Vietnamese jungles, and I wonder... Where was their safety and security.... and why were we there?

The Vietnam War was a tragedy. Nothing more, nothing less. The tragedy is that the greatest nation, the United States, a superpower, was humbled and defeated by its own ignorance and arrogance. The human side of this tragedy is of unspeakable proportions for those who fought and died there, and for those who suffer still. Vietnam was an immensely complex war. In South Vietnam, a country of sixty-seven thousand square miles, the war varied enormously from place to place and from year to year. A war that destroyed one presidency and all but consumed another managed to eliminate the national will and our sense of rightness for the American cause. It stands still today as a black haunting symbol of how *not* to execute a war or shape foreign policy.

We were in Vietnam "to protect South Vietnam's people from communist aggression." In our attempts to divert Ho Chi Minh and his cadres, the United States deployed 3.3 million American troops accompanied by an extreme application of firepower. Collectively, U.S. fliers dropped more than seven million tons of bombs on Indochina. That total was nearly three times the tonnage dropped in World War II and Korea combined! Although North Vietnam suffered incredible losses – around 600,000 dead – the United States suffered, as well. Fifty-eight thousand, two hundred fifty-six names are listed on the black walls of the Vietnam Veterans Memorial in Washington, D.C.; the latest addition of three names was added in 2007. For every twelve men killed in Southeast Asia, another was listed as a POW or MIA. In all, 4,833 men made that list. In 1976, three years after the Paris Peace Agreements were signed terminating American involvement in Vietnam, less than one in five of these men had been accounted for by the U.S. Where are these men and why could we not account for them?

We called our troops in Vietnam "murderers," "baby-killers," "psychedelic warriors." We spat in their faces as they returned home and welcomed them, not as the heroes they were, but as heinous objects that caused us disgust at the very sight of their being. We as a nation were more interested in LSD, demonstrations, rock bands, love-ins, and long hair, while men were dying by the thousands in a country most had never heard of and even more cared nothing about. Yet today, we can walk through the forests and open plains of this land with little fear of self-harm, and we owe that luxury to the men of Vietnam and of wars before and since.

In this complete world of ours, we take for granted what freedom means and how we acquired and now maintain that pleasure. Seldom do we stop and think about the men and women who served in the armed forces and paid with their lives, from one degree to another, in order that we the people remain free, safe, and protected from harm. Would you give up nearly six years of your life for a group of complete strangers? How about one or two years? Most wouldn't. Yet that is exactly what men like SSgt. Nathan Henry and thousands of others did because they felt it was their duty. And how many didn't come back at all? Over fifty-eight thousand men will never experience the joys of fatherhood or grandchildren. They will never walk their daughter down the aisle on her wedding day or congratulate a son at graduation. Never will they experience the freedoms offered by this great nation. The freedoms for which they gave their lives. The freedoms we take for granted.

So much was lost in Vietnam. Thousands of lives. Arms. Legs. Sight and Sanity. Innocence. Trust in a nation. Trust in a fellow American. Brothers, Fathers, husbands, sons. Best buddies, "short-timers" and "lifers." The women who served and won't return. Lost also is an era in time that if you remember it, you really weren't there. A time of William C. Westmoreland and The Beatles. "free-fire zones" and "body counts." Hell, no, we won't go. Kent State. The Rung Sat and the DMZ. Khe Sanh and My Lai. M-16's, pungi sticks, and "Willie P." AK47's and napalm. Speed trips and smoking a number. Hamlets, Ho Chi Minh, and Special Forces. Riots at home and "Where Have All the Flowers Gone." Peace. War. Cease-fire. .....And time.

Precious, irretrievable time was lost. For the POWs, especially, an exorbitant amount of time was forever lost within the boundaries of Indochina. For Nathan Henry, almost six years passed without knowledge of the outside world and the events that were taking place. Listed here are but a few of the more memorable events that occurred from the time he was captured until just after his return to the United States:

1967:
First heart transplant was performed
Freedom of Information Act goes into effect
Nguyen Van Thieu elected president of South Vietnam
Thurgood Marshall is sworn in as first black Supreme Court

justice

Thousands protesting the war in Vietnam try to storm the Pentagon

Singer Otis Redding dies in a plane crash at age 26

Wilt Chamberlain sets NBA record of twenty-two free throw misses

1968:

President Lyndon B. Johnson announces he will not seek re-election

Martin Luther King is assassinated

Bobby Kennedy is assassinated

Joe Frazier wins the heavyweight boxing title

Race riots breakout all over the United States

Mickey Mantle hits his last career homer #536

First Boeing 747 jet takes to the air

Jackie Kennedy marries Aristotle Onasis

Richard Nixon is elected president

First manned voyage to the moon occurs with Apollo 8

1969:

John Lennon and Yoko Ono shock the world with a nude album cover

The Concorde takes her maiden voyage

Golda Meir becomes prime minister of Israeli

Walt Disney World being construction in Florida

Neil Armstrong and Ed "Buzz" Aldrin are first men to walk on the moon

Manson murders occur

Woodstock opens in New York State

Vietnam Moratorium – millions nationwide protest the war

Joseph Kennedy dies

Apollo 12 takes 2 more Americans to the moon

U.S. holds first draft lottery since WWII

Beatles are the hottest rock group in the world

1970:

U.S. troops invade Cambodia

Four students are killed at Kent State
Willie Mays hits #3000
First computer chess set is introduced
Vince Lombardi dies at age fifty-seven
Janis Joplin and Jimi Hendrix die
Tom Dempsey, New Orleans Saints, kicks record NFL field goal
– sisty-three yards
USSR has first successful landing on Venus

1971:
Cigarette announcements banned on TV
U.S., UK, USSR, and others sign Sealed Treaty outlawing nuclear
weapons
Joe Frazier beats Muhammad Ali in Madison Square Gardens
Howard Hughes dies
Amtrak begins operations
Ed Sullivan has his final TV show
Louis Armstrong dies at age 71seventy-one
Billie Jean King becomes first female athlete to win $100,000

1972:
Hand-held calculators introduced at $395 each
Goodyear blimp takes maiden voyage
Arthur Godfrey ends twenty-seven years on radio
Watergate unravels
Olga Korbut wins Olympic gold in gymnastics
Mark Spitz becomes first athlete to win seven gold medals
Marcos declares martial law in Philippines
Jackie Robinson dies
Kissinger declares "peace is at hand" in Vietnam
Nixon wins second term
Apollo 17, last of Apollo Moon series, is launched
Heaviest bombing yet in Vietnam begins in Hanoi

1973:
Lyndon B. Johnson dies at age sixty-four
Edward G. Robinson dies at age eighty-two
George Foreman beats Joe Frazier for heavyweight boxing title

U.S. and Vietnam sign cease-fire agreement
First U.S. POWs released – 116 men
Last known remaining POWs released from Hanoi
Last combat troops leave Vietnam after nine years at war
Secretariat wins the Triple Crown

The United States made numerous mistakes concerning the Vietnam War. She faltered when the pressure was on and reverted to political games while using the lives of our servicemen as Her pawns. Mistakes are made on a daily basis by every human creature that inhabits this universe, and it should be our greatest desire that, through time and experience, these mistakes will be carefully analyzed and not repeated again.... especially within the arena of war. Yet even with Her flaws, the United States remains a proud and free country, and this writer counts her blessings daily to live within such a great nation. There is no reason to cover truths about the past. Hopefully within these pages, the Henry family has revealed additional truths through the first-hand knowledge of a man who was there and through documents saved from nearly thirty years ago. It is highly unlikely that most hidden truths will ever be revealed concerning the Vietnam War. People want to forget and bury the pain, the humiliation, the "unknowns," and go forth in their daily lives. Vietnam is not a war we should forget, but utilize what we learned to avoid making the same mistakes in future military encounters. We can only hope.

As I stood at the bottom of the steps leading to Nat's house, the book almost finished and preparing to leave, I took one last look at the man with whom I had spent so much time. He was bent over the railing of his deck, elbows propped and supporting his chin on his hands as they clasped together. A lit cigarette was held between his fingers, its smoke curling slowly around his face, embracing his thoughts and clouding his vision. Nat's eyes slowly and thoughtfully looked over the land that gracefully surrounded his home, and it seemed that once again he was lost in his own thoughts for a few precious seconds. Tears welled up and burned my eyes, as my heart filled instantly with an overwhelming feeling of pride mixed with empathy for this man. The words have been written and people now know most of the trials Nat faced during his captivity in Vietnam.

I couldn't help but think, though, that even with the most carefully selected words from the English language, no one would ever know, or be able to portray, the ghosts that haunted this gentle giant among men. It is my sincerest hope that I was able to do honorable justice to Nat's memory of his experiences as an enlisted man in the United States Army and as a Prisoner of War in Vietnam. My heart goes out to him, his family, and to what he has demonstrated as an indescribable level of courage, dedication and loyalty that represents the epitome of American patriotism. Nat, may your life be filled with peace, your nights embraced in quiet slumber, and may your name always be remembered as one who gave his all so the rest of us can enjoy life, liberty, and the pursuit of happiness within the vast boundaries of the greatest nation on earth..... The United States of America.

Author Bio

Beth W. Vinson was born in Atlanta, Georgia and grew up on a rolling farm in Franklin, North Carolina. She became a buff of the Vietnam Conflict through a marriage, numerous interviews with veterans, and extensive resea rch over several years. Her first manuscript, From Metal to Flesh, became the catalyst for To Hell and Beyond when Nathan Henry, a former Vietnam POW, read a section of the raw manuscript. Mr. Henry asked if Beth could write his story, and from that a friendship evolved and a tremendously moving account of life as a Prisoner of War in Vietnam.

Beth presently works as a Department of Defense contractor for the United States Navy in the role of Strategic Communications Manager. She previously published a marketing manual with her alma mater, Western Carolina University, but To Hell and Beyond is her first published book. She is single and currently lives in Norfolk, Virginia.

Purchase:

TO HELL AND BEYOND

The first enlisted man's version of what happened as
a Prisoner of War in Vietnam

Author: Beth W. Vinson
Copyright: 2008

To Hell and Beyond portrays the true story of torture, imprisonment, and
the barbarous acts inflicted upon a man few people would ever know. He,
and the other enlisted men who spent time as Prisoners of War, were not
known to the general public simply because they weren't highly decorated
pilots or thrust into the limelight during Operation Homecoming in 1973.
This is the story of one man who defied all odds to survive and who,
through recalling painful memories, will lead the reader step-by-step into
the horrors and debilitation suffered by him and all our men while held
as POWs during the Vietnam conflict. This manuscript, although based
on one man, reveals the pride and determination of all POWs and their
struggle to survive the tortures inflicted by the enemy in an effort to break
their spirits and turn them against the country that had sent them to the
Godforsaken jungles of Vietnam. This is the personal story of Nathan B.
Henry and his journey *To Hell and Beyond*.

Pages: 168
ISBN: 978-1-934937-28-0
ISBN-10: 1-934937-28-2

Visit our website at http://tohellandbeyond.com or contact the author
directly at bvnadmin@bvnservices.com for an autographed copy of this
moving experience through the jungles of Vietnam.

Price: $16.95 (USD)
S&H: $3.50 (domestic)
VA Sales Tax add: 5%

Use PayPal for your convenience at: http://tohellandbeyond.com!

Printed in the United States
128764LV00002B/1-174/P